LOVE AND ITS FRUITS

LOVE AND ITS
FRUITS

JONATHAN EDWARDS'
CHARITY AND ITS FRUITS
A PRACTICAL EXPOSITION OF 1 CORINTHIANS 13
SUMMARIZED FOR THE 21ST CENTURY

DANIEL CHAMBERLIN

FREE
GRACE
PRESS

Love and Its Fruits: A Practical Exposition of
1 Corinthians 13

Published by

Free Grace Press
815 Exchange Ave., Ste. 101
Conway, AR 72032
(501) 214-9663
email: support@freegracepress.com
website: www.freegracepress.com

Printed in the United States of America

Scripture quotations are taken from the King James Version of the Bible. Public domain.

ISBN: 978-1-952599-56-9

CONTENTS

Introduction

The value of Edwards' treatise on the thirteenth chapter of the First Epistle to the Corinthians is multifaceted. It expounds true religion in its most practical expression. It brings us to the heart of God. It examines our heart. It presents a convincing argument for the cessation of the apostolic gifts that is much needed in our day.

Several years ago, I was asked to write this summary for translation purposes. It was published in Spanish in 2007. My prayer is that English readers also will find it beneficial.

The original was first published in 1852, nearly a hundred years after the death of its author. His great-grandson, Tryon Edwards, edited the treatise. The irregularity of style that you may notice in the outlines from one chapter to another simply reflects the original.

I extend heartfelt thanks to those who have helped with proofreading and suggestions: Penny Golden, Michelle Starr, and my wife, Susan.

May the God of love be with you as you read!

Daniel Chamberlin
Wilderness Lodge
July 16, 2020

1

Love the Sum of All Virtue

Though I speak with the tongues of men and of angels, and have not charity, I am become as sounding brass, or a tinkling cymbal. And though I have the gift of prophecy, and understand all mysteries, and all knowledge; and though I have all faith, so that I could remove mountains, and have not charity, I am nothing. And though I bestow all my goods to feed the poor, and though I give my body to be burned, and have not charity, it profiteth me nothing.
— 1 Corinthians 13:1–3

The words of our text indicate that love is a matter of special and peculiar importance. This virtue is more insisted on than any other in all the New Testament. Charity by definition means love, or that disposition or affection whereby one is dear to another. This word *charity* speaks of Christian love in its full extent, whether exercised toward God or man.

The great doctrine taught here is that *all grace or virtue which comes to a person in salvation, and which distinguishes Christians from others, is summed up in this one quality called* love. So vital is love, that without it, all other qualities avail nothing. Love is the great thing, and all other virtues are contained or implied in it.

I. The nature of Christian love

All true Christian love is one and the same in its principle. Regardless of its object, its degree, and its mode of expression, the spring of this love ascends from one single fountain. Thus, it is distinguished from other inferior loves, which arise from various principles, motives, and views.

It is one Holy Spirit who influences the heart of a Christian in all the different aspects of this virtue. His work is one single work, causing us at once to love both God and man. Furthermore, every facet of Christian love springs from one motive: love for God and His excellency, beauty, and holiness. We love fallen men because they were created in the image and likeness of God. We love redeemed men because they are increasingly becoming more like God. Love to God is the foundation of gracious love to men.

II. Proof that Christian love is the sum of all virtue

Reason teaches us this truth. The very nature of love disposes a man to all proper acts of respect to both God and man. No other encouragement is needed. Love will dispose us to honor, worship, believe, and obey God. Love disposes us to act like a child toward our heavenly Father. A soul that loves God will delight to see self abased and God exalted. Toward our fellow-man, love disposes us to every good behavior, such as honesty, meekness, gentleness, and mercy. Love will keep us from enmity, cruelty, and selfishness. "Love worketh no ill to his neighbor" (Rom. 13:10). It disposes us to fulfill our God-given duties in all our earthly callings and relationships. If the principle of love be implanted in the heart, it alone is sufficient to produce all good practice, for it comprises every virtue.

Again, reason teaches that without love, all performances or apparent virtues are defective and hypocritical. Obedience without love is insincere and vain. He that does not love God will not respect Him nor trust Him. Without love, all good outward conduct is empty hypocrisy.

Scripture teaches us that love is the sum of all virtue. All that the Scripture requires of man is summed up in this one virtue. "He that loveth another hath fulfilled the law. . . . Love is the fulfilling of the law" (Rom. 13:8, 10). Love leads us to obey all of the Ten Commandments. All our moral duties are comprehended in the commands to love God and to love our neighbor (Matt. 22:37–40).

Since love is the sum of all our duty, it must be the sum of all real virtue.

The fact that faith works by love (Gal. 5:6) teaches us that love is the sum of all virtue. Faith produces good works, and the good works it produces are by love. Therefore, of necessity, love is an essential and distinguishing element in true, living faith. Love is no ingredient in a speculative faith, but is the life and soul of a practical faith. The former consists only in an assent of the understanding, the latter in the consent of the heart. The faith of devils is without any love, but love is the most essential factor in true faith. So allied are faith and love, that the consent of the heart cannot be distinguished from the love of the heart. "Whosoever believeth that Jesus is the Christ is born of God: and every one that loveth him that begat loveth him also that is begotten of him" (1 John 5:1). To the unbelieving Jews, our Lord could say, "Ye have not the love of God in you" (John 5:42).

All Christian obedience is called "the obedience of faith" (Rom. 16:26). Seeing that whatever this faith does it does *by love*, we can say that love encompasses all our duties toward God and man.

Now let us apply this truth to ourselves.

1. Self-Examination

What do we know of this love? Do we have it toward God and toward our fellow-man, especially those who are children of God? Do our daily lives exemplify a spirit of love like that which dwelt in the Lord Jesus Christ? "Hereby perceive we the love of God, because he laid down his life for us: and we ought to lay down our lives for the brethren. But whoso hath this world's good, and seeth his brother have need, and shutteth up his bowels of compassion from him, how dwelleth the love of God in him? My little children, let us not love in word, neither in tongue; but in deed and in truth. And hereby we know that we are of the truth, and shall assure our hearts before him" (1 John 3:16–19).

2. Instruction

This doctrine shows us what is the right Christian spirit. When the disciples wanted to call down fire from heaven upon the Samaritans, our Lord rebuked them saying, "Ye know not what manner of spirit ye are of" (Luke 9:55). He is not saying that they were ignorant of their own desires, but rather that they were ignorant of the spirit and temper that was proper for a Christian. They showed their ignorance of the true nature of Christ's kingdom–a kingdom of love and peace. So eminent is the grace of love that it may be called *the* Christian virtue. The gospel is full of love: love among the Persons of the Trinity, and love for unworthy sinners. Believers are repeatedly taught and exhorted to love God, love the brethren, and even love their enemies.

So necessary is love, that our whole profession may be tested by the presence or absence of this virtue. A spiritual knowledge of truth will always be accompanied by love in the soul, aimed toward God and every proper object. It is inconceivable that a person should have a true knowledge of God and be void of love for Him.

Herein is the beauty of a Christian spirit. The spirit of love is the spirit of heaven itself.

Herein is the happiness of a Christian life. A life of love is a pleasant life.

Here we learn why strife and discord tend so much to ruin true religion. Godliness and contention cannot live together. Religion suffers in times of contention among its professors.

It behooves every Christian to carefully guard against envy, malice, and bitterness. These attitudes contradict all that we profess. We must avoid the very first motion of such sins. Anything that hinders our love to men, will also hinder our love to God, for as we have seen, all Christian love is one single principle.

The command to love our enemies ought not to surprise us. This is the very sum of Christianity. This is the very spirit of Christ and of our heavenly Father: to love the worst enemies, even the chief of sinners.

3. Exhortation

Let us seek a spirit of love. Let us grow in it more and more. Let us abound in works of love. If you call yourself a Christian, where are your works of love? What have you done for God, for His glory, and for the advancement of His kingdom in the earth? What have you done for your fellow-man?

Do not excuse yourself by saying you have no opportunities. If your heart is full of love, it will find a way to vent itself in deeds. "My little children, let us not love in word, neither in tongue; but in deed and in truth" (1 John 3:18).

2

LOVE MORE EXCELLENT THAN THE EXTRAORDINARY GIFTS OF THE HOLY SPIRIT

Though I speak with the tongues of men and of angels, and have not charity, I am become as sounding brass, or a tinkling cymbal. And though I have the gift of prophecy, and understand all mysteries, and all knowledge; and though I have all faith, so that I could remove mountains, and have not charity, I am nothing.
— 1 Corinthians 13:1–2

In these verses, we see the comparison between love and the miraculous gifts. The apostolic age was an age of miracles. The church at Corinth was especially blessed with such gifts. However, the doctrine taught in our text by the inspired apostle is that *the ordinary influence of the Holy Spirit, working the grace of love in the heart, is a more excellent blessing than any of the extraordinary gifts of the Spirit.*

I. The distinction between gifts

One way to distinguish the various operations of the Spirit is to divide them into common and saving. Both believers and unbelievers receive some of the same gifts, such as a measure of knowledge, conviction of sin, gratitude, sorrow, and the like. These are common gifts. But there are other special, saving gifts which only the people redeemed by God receive, such as saving faith, love, peace, and the like.

The operations of the Spirit may also be divided into ordinary and extraordinary. The extraordinary gifts, such as tongues, miracles, and prophecy, were exceptional, only given in unusual occasions.

Their chief function was to reveal the mind of God to man before the written revelation was given. Since the written Word of God is now complete, these extraordinary gifts have ceased. On the other hand, the ordinary gifts, such as love, are given to every believer in every age, for their comfort and growth in holiness.

It is vital that we understand that these two divisions differ one from another. Ordinary graces are unique to the saints of God; they are not common gifts shared with unbelievers. Extraordinary gifts, however, were common, given to believers and unbelievers alike on many occasions. "Many will say to me in that day, Lord, Lord, have we not prophesied in thy name? and in thy name have cast out devils? and in thy name done many wonderful works? And then will I profess unto them, I never knew you: depart from me, ye that work iniquity" (Matt. 7:22–23).

II. The greatness of the extraordinary gifts

It is a privilege to hear the Word of God, but it is a greater privilege to proclaim it, as did the prophets. To witness a miracle is great, but to work a miracle is even greater. Those endowed with such gifts are specially honored to be like Christ in His prophetic office. Twice over Daniel is called "greatly beloved," and therefore the recipient of prophetic insight (Dan. 9:23; 10:11). Darius, the Persian king, took notice of the "excellent spirit" in Daniel (6:3), which no doubt included the spirit of prophecy and inspiration. This spirit is said to have been *excellent*, indicating the special quality of these gifts. Moses was envied for his extraordinary gifts. John would have worshiped the angel that brought him the revelation on the isle of Patmos, had the angel consented. Let none despise the importance and privilege of these extraordinary gifts!

III. The surpassing excellence of the ordinary gifts

As great as the extraordinary gifts were, the ordinary influence of the Holy Spirit working the grace of love in the heart, is a far more excellent privilege. Since, as we have seen, love is the sum of all saving grace in the heart, it is greater than any and all miraculous and extraordinary gifts. Let us mark some reasons why this is so.

Ordinary gifts or graces are qualities which God implants within the very nature of a person. However, this is not the case with extraordinary gifts. They do not improve the basic nature of the man. The source of miracle-working power does not reside within the man himself. Extraordinary gifts are like a jewel which may outwardly adorn the body; but true graces enter into the soul itself, transforming it into a precious jewel.

The Holy Spirit communicates Himself more in ordinary graces than in extraordinary gifts. In the case of the latter, the possessor of the gifts may work some great outward sign, yet remain inwardly empty of the Spirit of God. But with graces, the third Person of the Trinity is imparted in holiness of nature, or sanctification. With ordinary grace, men become "partakers of the divine nature" (2 Peter 1:4).

In redemption, the image of God is restored in man, not by extraordinary gifts, but by ordinary graces. The likeness that Adam lost was a moral likeness. It cannot be restored in any other capacity than morally, that is, to be made holy, to have the mind of Christ. No matter how many miracles one may work, without holiness, he is not yet like God in the area that really matters.

Ordinary graces are higher privileges, more precious and more scarce, for they are only given to God's children. However, extraordinary gifts are often bestowed upon the unregenerate. Balaam had the gift of prophecy for a while, but was a wicked man. Likewise with King Saul. Judas Iscariot was able to "heal the sick, cleanse the lepers, raise the dead," and even "cast out devils" (see Matt. 10:1-8). Miracle-working is a gift God sometimes gives to those He hates, but graces are given only to His beloved ones.

Ordinary graces are infinitely more excellent because of their consequences. Eternal life is promised to those who have graces, but not to those who merely have extraordinary gifts. Therefore, our Lord taught the seventy disciples, "In this rejoice not, that the spirits are subject unto you; but rather rejoice, because your names are written in heaven" (Luke 10:20). Graces surpass gifts because graces have eternal life annexed to them.

Ordinary graces afford a higher degree of happiness. Man's highest happiness consists in holiness. If he possesses holiness, he can be happy without anything else. But no other possessions or privileges, like extraordinary gifts, will make him happy without this.

The ordinary sanctifying work of the Holy Spirit is the end or purpose of all the extraordinary gifts. The extraordinary gifts were given in order to propagate the gospel, that is, to make saints, and also to edify those saints, building them up in holiness. "And he gave some, apostles; and some, prophets; and some, evangelists," these extraordinary gifts being given for this end: "for the perfecting of the saints, for the work of the ministry, for the edifying of the body of Christ," which edifying is *in love* (Eph. 4:11, 12, 16). Since the end is always more excellent than the means, holiness is better than giftedness.

Extraordinary gifts existing alone, without true graces, will only serve to aggravate the condemnation of those who have them. Some of the apostates described in Hebrews chapter 6 evidently possessed great gifts. They "were made partakers of the Holy Ghost and tasted the good word of God, and the powers of the world to come." Thus, their condemnation was greater and their sentence more severe because of these privileges that they later credited to the devil.

Ordinary graces are better than extraordinary gifts because they will outlast them. Verse 8 of our text declares, "Charity never faileth: but whether there be prophecies, they shall fail; whether there be tongues, they shall cease; whether there be knowledge, it shall vanish away."

This leads us to the following practical considerations:

1. Since graces last forever, they are the greatest blessings God bestows upon a mortal in this world. They are even greater than the privilege of the miraculous conception. "It came to pass…a certain woman of the company lifted up her voice, and said unto him, Blessed is the womb that bare thee, and the paps which thou hast sucked. But he said, Yea rather, blessed are they that hear the word of God, and keep it" (Luke 11:27–28).

2. *The ordinary and extraordinary gifts must not be confused.* The latter are no sure sign of saving grace. Wonderful visions are no proofs of grace. The only way for a person to know if he is in a state of grace is to discern the hearty exercise of Christian love, which is the sum of all other virtues. Without this mark, other gifts prove nothing.

3. *If saving graces are more excellent than miracle-working, then there is no basis upon which to assume, as some do, that in a latter-day revival the extraordinary signs must return.* God's cause in the earth may well enjoy its most prosperous times without the presence of those gifts. We have no reason to expect the written revelation from God to be enlarged by new prophecies. The closing words of John's Revelation (22:18–21) make this clear.

4. *Those who possess ordinary graces have reason to be very thankful to God.* Let us not underestimate the tremendous privilege of being like Christ, and having His love in our hearts. What more could God do for us? Therefore, "What manner of persons ought we to be in all holy conversation and godliness?" (2 Peter 3:11). Our constant prayer should be, "What shall I render unto the LORD for all his benefits toward me?" (Ps. 116:12). Let us consider the high privileges that are ours, and humbly walk in the shadow of His love. Such love claims our best and our all.

5. *May those who are lost in sin seek these blessings of God's grace.* Consider your present misery in your affections for the emptiness of this world. Yet God has made you with a capacity to know Him and to enjoy His love. Multitudes have already been converted. Why do you not come to God through Christ and discover the riches of His grace?

3

GREATEST PERFORMANCES OR SUFFERINGS IN VAIN WITHOUT LOVE

And though I bestow all my goods to feed the poor,
and though I give my body to be burned,
and have not charity, it profiteth me nothing.
— 1 Corinthians 13:3

Having considered the extraordinary gifts and their emptiness apart from Christian love, the apostle now addresses matters of a moral nature. This verse mentions two items: first, our performances, such as giving all to the poor; and second, being burned as a martyr. Giving to the poor was a common and necessary deed in the early churches, due to persecution and to the demands put upon the many who evangelized full-time. In both his letters to the Corinthians, Paul speaks of their giving to the needy saints in Judea. Yet, here he tells them that they can give their all for this cause, and be profited nothing if they have not love. Then he mentions suffering of the most extreme kind, being consumed in the flames of persecution. Many at that time were called upon to give not only their goods, but also their bodies in agonizing death. Nevertheless, it would all be in vain if not accompanied with and springing from love, which, as we have seen, is the sum of distinguishing grace in the heart.

The doctrine set forth here is this: *all that men can do and suffer, can never make up for the lack of sincere Christian love in the heart.*

15

I. Great performances and great sufferings may exist without love.

This same apostle knew much about *great performances*. In Philippians 3, he lists some of his own that he did before his conversion. Likewise, we hear the Pharisee in Luke 18:11–12 rehearsing his performances as he prays. How many such performances are done without sincere love of heart, springing from motives such as a desire for fame, or fear of hell, or to appease God!

Also, consider what *great sufferings* have been endured without true Christian love. The Pharisees, and many Romanists after them, endured much self-torture voluntarily. Many pagans who refused to submit to the Romanists died as martyrs for their pagan beliefs. Many Muslims willingly laid down their lives in the crusades, in order to gain a better paradise. Yet none of these died with sincere divine love in their hearts. (But the number of martyrs for true Christianity swells beyond all these.)

II. Performances and sufferings cannot make up for the lack of love.

This is true for the following reasons:

External things in themselves are worth nothing in God's sight. Without a living principle of love within, all external actions are nothing more to God than the motions of inanimate matter. Our external obedience, apart from vital love, might as well be gold or pearls, which God has no need of whatsoever. He says, "For every beast of the forest is mine, and the cattle upon a thousand hills. . . . If I were hungry, I would not tell thee: for the world is mine, and the fulness thereof" (Ps. 50:10, 12). "For the LORD seeth not as man seeth; for man looketh on the outward appearance, but the LORD looketh on the heart" (1 Sam. 16:7). God is in no way profited by the sufferings of human beings. He is interested in the motive, purpose, and end of these sufferings.

Without the heart, nothing is truly given to God. Every act of worship must first involve the understanding, the affections, and the will. Otherwise there is only a mechanical movement, as if a musical instrument were playing by itself. Many actions considered to be worship really amount to a man worshiping himself, since the end in view is his own honor and profit. Such is a mockery to God, and gives Him nothing at all.

Love is the sum of all that God requires of us. It is absurd to imagine that anything can make up for the lack of the *sum* of all God requires. By withholding love, we withhold the totality of what God requires. It is absurd to think we could make up for one debt by paying another. It is more absurd to think we could make up for the whole debt by paying nothing whatsoever, and continuing to withhold what is required.

An outward show of love without true love in the heart is hypocrisy and a lie. All the flattery in the world cannot deceive God. We can never make up for the lack of truth by lying.

Without love, performances and sufferings are only offerings to some idol. That which is not truly offered to God, must be offered to someone or something. Whatever that is, it is an idol. What folly to imagine that we can make up for withholding worship from God by offering something to our idol! Would a wife make up for her lack of affection to her husband by giving her love to a stranger?

Let us now consider what we should learn from this truth.

1. We ought to examine ourselves.

Perhaps you have done much, and even suffered much, but the real question is, "Has your heart been sincere in it all, and have you done it all for God and His glory?" Certainly, every Christian knows something of the hypocrisy of his own heart, but is there any sincerity? Despite our hypocrisy, God looks for any sincerity. A cup of cold water given to a disciple in Christian love is worth more in God's sight than a whole kingdom given up to feed the poor, without this love.

Now let us mark four things necessary to sincerity. Sincerity consists of:

- *Truth.* What appears in the action must be truly in the heart. "Behold, thou desirest truth in the inward parts" (Ps. 51:6). This is to be "without guile" (John 1:47). Examine yourself: Is there only an appearance of love to God in your actions?

- Freedom. A Christian's obedience is that of a child, not of a slave. It is not forced from without, but it springs from within. Examine yourself: Have you chosen God for His own sake, because you delight in Him?

- Integrity. That is, a sincere heart is one wholly given to God. The whole body and soul must be united in the fear and service of God. Examine yourself: Is your every faculty yielded to the obedience of Christ, and brought in subjection to His will?

- Purity. We must have an opposition to sin that is unmixed, unadulterated. Examine yourself: Do you harbor some love for sin, or is your love to God sincere and pure?

2. Lost souls ought to be convicted.

Without a heart of love, renewed by regenerating grace, you may deny yourself and suffer ever so much, all to no avail. None of these things can atone for your sins or commend you to God. You would be glad to do something to make up for a lack of grace in your heart, but there is no substitute. Rest on nothing that you have done or suffered, but rather rest on Christ alone. Let your heart be filled with sincere love to Him as your all in all.

3. Believers ought to highly prize the presence of Christian love in their hearts.

Since this is the sum of all virtue, and since everything else is nothing without it, let us seek it with diligence and prayer. Only God can bestow such a disposition. We may be called upon to do and suffer much, but let us not rest in these actions. They are only outward evidences. A hearty love for God is the main thing, apart from which our best deeds only deepen our condemnation.

4

LOVE ENABLES US TO MEEKLY BEAR INJURIES FROM OTHERS

Charity suffereth long.
— 1 Corinthians 13:4

Now we come to consider the nature of Christian love by examining the apostle's description of its various amiable and excellent fruits. First in the list is this: *a truly Christian spirit will dispose us to meekly bear the evil that we receive from others.*

Longsuffering is part of the fruit of the Holy Spirit (Gal. 5:22), and Scripture repeatedly enjoins it upon believers. In Matthew 11:29, our Lord emphasized this quality which He manifests, and which we should learn from Him. "Learn of me; for I am meek and lowly in heart."

I. The various kinds of injuries given by others

We could compile an almost endless list of wrongs which are committed or might be committed against a person. Dishonesty in business transactions, oppression, unfair advantage, unfaithfulness to agreements, slander, premature and unfair judgment, contemptuous thoughts, willingness to believe the worst and to report it to others, abuse of authority, or else resistance against authority, selfishness, pride, malice, revenge, grudges, and the like. The natural

19

man hates others without a cause. He wickedly imagines that their fall is his own elevation.

II. What it is to meekly bear these injuries?

What is the nature of this duty?

Suffering long implies that we seek no revenge for the wrongs we suffer. We naturally desire to injure in some way those who injure us. This we call *revenge*. But Christian love seeks no revenge or retaliation, either in words or deeds. In the face of injury, we are called to gentleness, calmness, and peace. Even if the case requires that we reprove the offender, we must do so without bitterness and resentment, and we should show him that his offense is more against God than against us. We seek his good, not his harm.

Even more, suffering long means that we should maintain a right disposition of love toward the offender. We should not hate him because he has injured us. We may pity him, but not hate him.

Suffering long means that we do not lose the quietness and repose of our own minds and hearts when we have been injured. We must allow no injury to so disquiet us that we are not able to carry out our duties, especially the duties of secret religion in our souls. "In your patience possess ye your souls" (Luke 21:19).

In many cases, suffering long means to forego a lawful defending of ourselves and to endure injuries to our interests and feelings for the sake of peace. We must refuse in most cases to vindicate ourselves. Most often, this only leads to an injuring of the other party, and establishes a hostility that is seldom repaired. "Why do ye not rather take wrong? Why do ye not rather suffer yourselves to be defrauded?" (1 Cor. 6:7). We must allow for cases in which we must defend ourselves, and possibly cause others to suffer, but even then it should normally be only after we have borne long.

Why is it called "longsuffering" or suffering long?

The term implies not just a small injury, but a large one, or repeated ones. We are not to bear with our offending neighbor until we reach our limit. Rather, we are to continue to bear with him as long as his injuries continue, even to the end. In those cases where we have no choice but to defend ourselves, we should do so in a spirit of love, not of revenge or desire to injure him.

III. How love disposes us to meekly bear injuries

Love to God tends to make us willing to suffer long.

God Himself is longsuffering, and love disposes us to imitate Him. He declared this attribute to Moses in Exodus 34:6, "The Lord, The Lord God, merciful and gracious, longsuffering." It is called one of God's riches in Romans 2:4, "Despisest thou the riches of his goodness and forbearance and longsuffering?" Consider all the wickedness in this world, and then consider how patiently God bears with it, sending rain and giving food. He suffers long with sinners, to whom He offers His mercy, even while they are rebelling against Him. He is longsuffering to His elect until He brings them to repentance. Paul said that when he was known as Saul of Tarsus, Christ showed a pattern of all longsuffering toward him (1 Tim. 1:16). A loving heart will want to imitate this quality so marvelously manifested by God. As His children, we must follow our Father, and be longsuffering even as He is longsuffering.

Love also disposes us to express our gratitude for God's longsuffering toward us. The injuries others inflict on us are nothing in comparison with those we heaped up against God. If we refuse to suffer long with our neighbors, we are practically disapproving of God's longsuffering with us.

Love to God tends to produce true humility, which is one main root of a longsuffering spirit. In humility, we have a deep sense of our own vileness, and our unworthiness of any good. He that is small in his own eyes, will not think as much of an injury as does one who has great thoughts of self. Pride is the foundation of a spirit of resentment and revenge.

Love to God enables us to regard the hand of God in the injuries we suffer, and to submit to His will. Truly, we see God's hand in everything, and we know His purpose is just and kind. Thus, David could suffer long with the cursing of Shimei. "Let him curse, because the LORD hath said unto him, Curse David" (2 Sam. 16:10).

In a sense, love to God sets us above any injury that men might inflict upon us. Our life is hid with Christ in God (Col. 3:3). All things work together for our good (Rom. 8:28). All things end up being for us. The more we are wrapped up in loving God, the less earthly injuries will be able to touch our spirits. Since our hearts are not set on worldly interests, and since these are the only things our enemies can touch, injuries come to be hardly worthy of the name.

Love to our neighbor tends to make us willing to suffer long.

As Proverbs 10:12 states, "Love covereth all sins." A parent bears many offenses from his child which he would not bear from another's child. Why? Because of his heart of love for his own. Likewise, Christian love teaches us to meekly bear all the injuries we receive from others. Let us mention several motives to this end.

The example of Christ moves us to longsuffering. Look at Him in His incarnation and earthly ministry, as the subject of contempt and reproach on the part of the very ones He came to save. He was called a Samaritan and demon-possessed. He was charged with drunkenness and blasphemy, and of being in affinity with publicans and sinners. His enemies hated Him with a mortal hatred, often conspiring His death. Yet how long was His longsuffering! Not one word of bitterness fell from His lips, even in the torture and shame before His crucifixion. Listen to Him as He prays for the forgiveness of those who nailed Him to the cross! Nothing could interrupt His longsuffering. We ought to love our worst neighbors as did our Lord.

If we are not prepared to suffer long, we are not fit to live at all in this world, for in it we meet with many injuries from our fellow-man. Our world is a fallen world—corrupt, miserable, under the dominion of sin. God's children walk "as sheep in the midst of wolves" (Matt. 10:16). If we do not have a longsuffering disposition, we will be continually upset and in perpetual turmoil. We should not be surprised by trials as though some strange thing is happening to us (1 Peter 4:12).

Longsuffering enables a Christian to live above injuries. Instead of being conquered by them, he conquers them. In proportion as we allow our minds to be disturbed by offenses, we fall under their power. However, our enemies are frustrated when they see our serenity of soul.

Longsuffering is a mark of true greatness of soul. "He that is slow to anger is better than the mighty; and he that ruleth his spirit than he that taketh a city" (Prov. 16:32). It is a small mind that is easily unsettled by man's ill-treatment, like a small stream is troubled by obstacles and is noisy as it passes over them. But a mighty river passes over the same calmly and quietly.

Longsuffering is commended by the best examples of saints before us. We have mentioned the example of our Lord, but let us also note men of like passions as ourselves, such as David when suffering at the hands of Saul. He refused the advice of his friends and spared the king's life more than once, committing himself into God's protection. Or think of Stephen who, like his Lord, prayed for his murderers' pardon with his last breath. Paul is a prime example of suffering at the hands of his enemies, yet maintaining a longsuffering disposition. Church history is full of more examples.

If we would be rewarded with God's longsuffering, we must be longsuffering toward others. "With the merciful thou wilt shew thyself merciful" (Ps. 18:25). "For if ye forgive men their trespasses, your heavenly Father will also forgive you: But if ye forgive not men their trespasses, neither will your Father forgive your trespasses" (Matt. 6:14–15). Are we not conscious of how much we need God's longsuffering and love for our many injuries against Him? Then let us demonstrate the same graciousness toward those who injure us.

Now, let us consider some objections that might be raised against this duty.

"The injuries I have received are intolerable. Flesh and blood cannot bear them."

But are these injuries worse than those you have committed against God, who is the Author of all mercies, and to whom you are under the highest obligation? Do you hope that God will bear long with your sins, and that Christ will embrace you in His dying love to pardon all your offenses? Do you approve of God's suffering long with you, or would you have liked Him better if He had instead cut you off long ago in His wrath? If you approve of this quality in God, why do you not approve of it in yourself? Is it less evil for you to offend the living God of heaven, than for a man to offend you? Why should you pray to God for pardon, while refusing to pardon your offender? Are you willing for God to pardon you the same way you pardon your fellow-man? Did Christ turn in revenge against His enemies while on this earth? Have you not trodden Him under foot more than others have trodden you under foot? Whose transgression is the greater?

"Those who have injured me have not repented, but persist in their injuries."

What occasion would there be for longsuffering, were not the offense to last long? Who ever heard of short longsuffering! How else can God test your longsuffering? And has He not suffered long with your obstinate and persistent injuries?

"If I suffer long, my enemies will only be encouraged in their injuries. I will only be injured all the more."

Do you know what the future holds with respect to the hearts of your enemies? Is not God more able than you to put a stop to the wrath of man? Experience proves that longsuffering tends more to put an end to injuries, while seeking revenge provokes more injuries. Prize the spirit of longsuffering, and you shall possess your soul in patience and happiness.

5
Love Inclines Us to Do Good

Charity . . . is kind.
— 1 Corinthians 13:4

Not only does Christian love cause us to bear all injuries, it goes beyond that. The phrase in our present text indicates that it also *disposes us freely to do good to others.*

I. The nature of doing good to others

It involves good actions. Certainly, the best way of doing good to others is by doing good to their souls. Doing spiritual and eternal good for someone is better than to give them the riches of the universe. How may we do such good to souls? By instructing them in the knowledge of God and truth. By encouraging and exhorting them concerning their personal duty before God. By reproving and warning those that are walking in the wrong path. By setting an example worth following, which is usually the most effectual method of all. Furthermore, saints may comfort, establish, and strengthen one another in faith and obedience, especially in seasons of temptation, trial, and a dull frame of mind.

Other opportunities of doing good to others arise in the outward aspects of this world. All men are subject to many kinds of tempo-

27

ral calamities. Our Lord listed some in the twenty-fifth chapter of Matthew: hunger, thirst, homelessness, nakedness, sickness, and imprisonment. Such circumstances are occasions for showing Christian kindness. We may also do good by defending someone's good name, or adding to their true comfort and happiness in this world in any way. These deeds and words of kindness tend to open doors for doing them higher spiritual good. Temporal good, whether giving, helping, or suffering, reinforces the spiritual good. "Bear ye one another's burdens, and so fulfil the law of Christ" (Gal. 6:2).

It involves good actions toward all. Scripture often employs the term *neighbor* as the one to whom we ought to do good. When asked, "Who is my neighbor?" our Lord answered with the parable of the good Samaritan who helped a Jew. This parable concerning two groups known for their mutual hatred, instructs us in the following points.

First, we should do good both to the good and the bad. God Himself "sendeth rain on the just and on the unjust" (Matt. 5:45). We owe a special duty to do good toward those "who are of the household of faith," according to Galatians 6:10. Yet our duty does not end with fellow-saints. The same verse instructs us to "do good to all men, as we have opportunity." If we withhold our good from the proud, covetous, immoral, profane members of society, we will lose our opportunity to benefit them in spiritual things and win them to Christ.

Second, we should do good both to friends and enemies. We hardly need to be instructed concerning the former, but toward the latter we are instructed by our Lord. "I say unto you, Love your enemies, bless them that curse you, do good to them that hate you, and pray for them which despitefully use you, and persecute you" (Matt. 5:44). Likewise, we are exhorted, "Recompense to no man evil for evil" (Rom. 12:17).

Third, we should do good both to the thankful and the unthankful. God "is kind unto the unthankful" (Luke 6:35). If we excuse ourselves by saying, "I will not do good to those who show themselves unthankful," we have not sufficiently looked at Christ. We betray either an ignorance of Christian duty or an unwillingness to obey.

It involves a right manner. The very nature of kindness demands that we demonstrate it *freely*, not expecting any reward or return. "Do good, and lend, hoping for nothing again" (Luke 6:35). We must do good *cheerfully* and heartily, with genuine goodwill toward others, "without grudging" (1 Peter 4:9; Rom. 12:8). We should also do good in a liberal and bountiful manner. "Thou shalt open thine hand wide" unto the poor (Deut. 15:8). The apostle encouraged the Corinthians to "sow bountifully" toward the needy saints in Judea (2 Cor. 9:6).

II. The disposition of doing good to others.

Goodwill toward others is the main ingredient in love. This is called *love of benevolence*, or the desire for good to be enjoyed by the beloved one. There is also the *love of complacence*, or the desire for good to be enjoyed in the beloved one. But the former is the main thing in Christian love. It reflects the love of God Himself who declared through the angel, "good will toward men" (Luke 2:14).

The most proper and conclusive evidence of love is that it effectually works. The test of a true desire to do good for someone is to do it! The proper and conclusive evidence of the will is the act, when there is power to act. Sincerity of desire leads not to mere words of benevolence, but deeds of benevolence. "My little children, let us not love in word, neither in tongue; but in deed and in truth" (1 John 3:18). James 2:16 exposes the hypocrisy that only says, "Depart in peace, be ye warmed and filled."

Now let us make some applications of this truth to our own hearts.

1. Reproof

All those who are not kind, not benevolent, and who do not freely do good to others are hereby reproved, for this is the truly Christian spirit. Certainly, a malicious Christian is an utter contradiction. A selfish Christian is a contradiction. Christian love extends to all our practices. Take, for example, our business transactions. We ought not overcharge for our goods or services, nor refuse to pay others what theirs are worth. Such pinching and grinding is evidence of selfishness. The rule for the child of God is to do to others as we would have them do to us.

2. Exhortation

Let us do good to others, endeavoring to be a blessing to them for time and for eternity. Let our benevolence be universal, constant, free, habitual, and according to our opportunity and ability.

Consider what a great honor it is to be an instrument of good in the world. God's blessing upon Abraham included that he would "be a blessing" (Gen. 12:2). Christ taught that even among the Gentiles great men are called "benefactors" (Luke 22:25). Christian benefactors are like God Himself, who pours out His blessings on mankind.

When others are disposed to do good to us, we most highly approve of their conduct. What we thus approve in others, let us exemplify ourselves. Again, this is simply obeying the rule of Christ to love others as ourselves.

Consider how kind God is to us. His temporal blessings are great, but how much more His eternal blessings! He has given us more than all the kingdoms of the earth; He has given us His only-begotten and well-beloved Son, the greatest gift He could bestow. In behalf of us who were evil and unthankful enemies, this Son came and suffered freely, without grudging, and without hope of reward.

Consider the great rewards promised to those that freely do good to others. Scarcely any other duty enjoined upon God's people has so many promises annexed to it as does this one. "With the merciful thou wilt shew thyself merciful" (Ps. 18:25). "It is more blessed to give than to receive" (Acts 20:35); that is, the giver is more happy in parting with his goods than is the receiver in taking them. "He that hath pity upon the poor lendeth unto the LORD; and that which he hath given will he pay him again" (Prov. 19:17). "He that giveth unto the poor shall not lack: but he that hideth his eyes shall have many a curse" (Prov. 28:27). "Blessed is he that considereth the poor: the LORD will deliver him in time of trouble" (Ps. 41:1). "Give, and it shall be given unto you; good measure, pressed down, and shaken together, and running over, shall men give into your bosom. For with the same measure that ye mete withal it shall be measured to you again" (Luke 6:38). "When thou makest a feast, call the poor, the maimed, the lame, the blind: And thou shalt be blessed; for they cannot recompense thee: for thou shalt be recompensed at the resurrection of the just" (Luke 14:13–14). The word from Christ to those who are kind is, "Come, ye blessed of my Father, inherit the kingdom prepared for you from the foundation of the world: For I was an hungred, and ye gave me meat: I was thirsty, and ye gave me drink: I was a stranger, and ye took me in: Naked, and ye clothed me: I was sick, and ye visited me: I was in prison, and ye came unto me. . . . Inasmuch as ye have done it unto one of the least of these my brethren, ye have done it unto me" (Matt. 25:34–36, 40).

6

LOVE INCONSISTENT WITH
AN ENVIOUS SPIRIT

Charity . . . envieth not.
— 1 Corinthians 13:4

Now we consider the tendency of Christian love with respect to good possessed by others. *Love, or a truly Christian spirit, is the opposite of an envious spirit.*

I. The nature of envy

Envy may be defined as dissatisfaction with, and opposition to, the prosperity and happiness of others as compared with our own. Every man naturally loves to be uppermost, higher than others. We cannot bear seeing others above us in honor or enjoyment. Self must be superior!

Envy is manifest in an uneasiness and dissatisfaction with the prosperity of others. We ought to rejoice in their prosperity. Instead, envy leaves us unable to enjoy even what we have. Like Haman, in spite of our present riches and honor, we still say, "Yet all this availeth me nothing, so long as I see Mordecai the Jew sitting at the king's gate" (Est. 5:13). Envy delights to see the prosperity of others diminished, and is often willing to lend a hand to that end.

33

How often are bitter words uttered in hopes of lowering the esteem of one in the eyes of others!

Envy is manifest in a dislike of others' very persons because of their prosperity. The envious person hates his neighbors for no other reason than the fact that they prosper. Joseph's brothers so envied his place of honor, "they hated him, and could not speak peaceably unto him" (Gen. 37:4). Sometimes, like these brothers, embittered people are prepared to destroy not only the envied one's happiness but also his very life.

II. Wherein a Christian spirit of love is the opposite of an envious spirit

Love disallows the exercise and expressions of envy. Though the sin of envy still indwells him, the Christian recognizes it as sin, and fights against it in his soul. He hates it in himself as well as in others. He makes every effort to keep it from breaking out in words and actions.

Love also tends to crucify the principle of envy in the motions of the heart. The disposition of envy must be mortified at its very root. In its place, love promotes a spirit of contentment with whatever lot God has appointed us. "I have learned, in whatsoever state I am, therewith to be content" (Phil. 4:11).

Love disposes us to rejoice in the prosperity of others. Love enables us to "rejoice with them that do rejoice" (Rom. 12:15). Such a spirit of goodwill casts out the spirit of envy, leaving room only for happiness in seeing our neighbor's success.

III. The reason and evidence of this doctrine

The Scriptures expressly speak against envy. The New Testament is full of precepts of goodwill to others. Furthermore, we read many particular warnings against the sin of envy. Envy is a mark of carnality. "For whereas there is among you envying, and strife, and divisions, are ye not carnal, and walk as men?" Envy is ranked among the abominable "works of the flesh," alongside murder and drunkenness. Envy is one of the hateful sins in which we lived before our conversion, but from which we have been redeemed, and which we must forsake. James connects envy with "every evil work," being "earthly, sensual, devilish." (1 Cor. 3:3; Gal. 5:21; Titus 3:3; James 3:15-16.)

The doctrines and history of the gospel speak against envy. In the gospel, the triune God, far from envying man, elevates him to the highest position of which human nature is capable. God the Father withheld nothing good from us, nor begrudged us His dearest thing–His only-begotten Son. And think of the Son Himself, who did not begrudge us anything He could do for us or give to us. He gave His incarnate life and blood. He has even determined to share His glory with His people forever. How different this is from Satan, who envied mankind's original happiness and honor, and labored to destroy it! Yet Christ came to destroy this destruction, to purify us, and to make us fit for heaven.

The self-denial of Christ and His promotion of His people all speak the opposite of a spirit of envy. He lived in lowly circumstances, submitted Himself to John's baptism, refused to be made an earthly king, and promised to His disciples that they would do greater works than He had done (which in the book of Acts came to pass).

The true spirit of Christian love will enable us to yield to these precepts. Christian love is directly contrary to envy. If we truly love our neighbor, we will not be unhappy at his good fortune. More generally, love prompts us to submit to God's authority, to obey His commands, and to imitate Christ's example in these things. Love makes a rather indirect assault against envy by mortifying pride, which is the ultimate source of envy. Love tends to work humility in our hearts, as we shall see in the next chapter.

Now let us apply this subject.

1. Self-examination

In time past, have you seen others prospering while you have long borne your burdens? How did these arrangements affect you? Were you dissatisfied? Did you wish to see the others brought down? Have you harbored ill will toward them? How often have our hearts burned with envy toward others!

In time present, do you see a brother or sister week after week in God's house, whose prosperity is an eyesore to you? Would you find it comforting if they should suddenly be brought low? But it is not just the lowly who need to examine their hearts. Those who presently prosper must consider whether they despise the thought of others gaining on them. Do you detest others when they narrow the margin between you and them, lest they should get above you? Is not a spirit of envy more with us than we realize or wish to admit?

Perhaps you call envy by another name, so as to justify it. One may say, *I deserve more honor than my neighbor, so I am not really envious.* But is there an envious man anywhere who does not so reason? Again, *My neighbor is unworthy of such honor.* But is it your neighbor's faults that trouble you, or is it really his prosperity? If it is his faults, why do you complain to others about him, and not rather try to help him? *But my neighbor makes poor use of his prosperity and honor. He needs to be humbled.* Be honest and ask yourself if your lamentations over his prosperity stem from pity for his soul, or from envy because you want what he has. Do not deceive yourself.

Do you sometimes envy others of their spiritual prosperity and graces? This is a great evil which ought never to be. Yet it has often raised its ugly head, as in the case of Cain and Abel.

2. Mortification

We must disallow and put away everything that resembles an envious spirit. Do you profess to be a Christian? Prove it by exercising love that envies not! "Who is a wise man and endued with knowledge among you? let him shew out of a good conversation his works with meekness of wisdom. But if ye have bitter envying and strife in your hearts, glory not, and lie not against the truth" (James 3:13-14).

An envious man is like a caterpillar: he delights in devouring the most flourishing trees and plants. He eats like a cancer. "A sound heart is the life of the flesh: but envy the rottenness of the bones" (Prov. 14:30). It is a most foolish and self-destructive spirit to a man. The prosperity of others harms him none whatsoever, yet he cannot enjoy what he has, because he sees others enjoying what they have. Even worse, the envious soul is like the Devil himself. Envy is the disposition of hell, and is the very opposite of the disposition of heaven. A Christian spirit leads us to always rejoice in the welfare of others.

A Spirit of Love Is
a Humble Spirit

Charity vaunteth not itself, is not puffed up,
doth not behave itself unseemly.
— 1 Corinthians 13:4–5

The previous phrase dealt with how a spirit of love behaves with respect to the good possessed by others. The present phrases deal with how a spirit of love behaves with respect to the good possessed by ourselves. As Christian love prevents us from envying others, so it also keeps us from boasting. It teaches us how to conduct ourselves properly, whether we be below or above others. Of course, this principle deals not only with our actions, but also with our whole inner disposition. *The doctrine here is that love is not proud but humble.*

I. Humility defined

Humility may be defined as a habit of mind and heart corresponding to our unworthiness and vileness before God, or our comparative lowness in His sight, with a behavior answering to such a state.

We must have a sense of our comparative lowness. We say *comparative* lowness, because humility is a grace befitting to creatures who are glorious and excellent in many respects. The glorified spirits in heaven are free from sin, but still have much reason to be humble before the Almighty God. God Himself is not humble, for that would involve some finiteness in Him. Neither pride nor humility are among His attributes. The humiliation of the Son of God refers to His incarnate state, and to His human nature in particular. Humility is an excellence fitting to all creatures, whether unfallen or fallen.

Humility consists chiefly in a sense of the infinite distance between God and ourselves. We are little and despicable creatures, even worms of the dust. Compared to God, we should feel that we are nothing and less than nothing. In a high moment of intercession, Abraham remembered his whole position before God, saying, "Behold now, I have taken upon me to speak unto the Lord, which am but dust and ashes" (Gen. 18:27). This spirit is essential to true humility. We may humble ourselves before certain of our fellow-men, but still remain proud before God. Thus, many who appear humble because of their earthly circumstances are nonetheless void of the true grace of humility.

In comparison with many others around us, we have reason to be humble. But for this humility to be true, it must arise from a sense of our lowness before God. Seeing our true position before our Creator will help us to assume a proper position before our fellow-creatures. Even before sin entered the human race, humility was a virtue. Adam was conscious of his smallness, weakness, dependence on God, and submission to God. This would keep him from pride among his fellow-creatures.

Since the fall of Adam, our cause for humility is much greater. Now not only are we naturally low but morally so as well. We are worse than creatures; we are vile, filthy, sinful creatures. This in particular is what convicts the conscience before God: a knowledge of our moral distance from Him. He is high and holy, but we are low and vile. This knowledge led Isaiah to cry out, "Woe is me!" (Isa. 6:5). It led Job to abhor himself (Job 42:6). Upon such a soul, our Lord pronounces a blessing in the first beatitude, "Blessed are the poor in spirit: for theirs is the kingdom of heaven" (Matt. 5:3). We need a sight, not only of His greatness, but also of His loveliness. The fallen angels see His greatness but not His beauty. We must recognize how unworthy we are of His goodness and grace. With Jacob we confess, "I am not worthy of the least of all the mercies, and of all the truth, which thou hast shewed unto thy servant" (Gen. 32:10). With David we confess, "Who am I, O Lord God? and what is my house, that thou hast brought me hitherto?" (2 Sam. 7:18).

We must have a disposition to conduct ourselves according to this sense of our lowness. This is the acid test of humility: Do we merely sense our lowness, or do we comply with its demands, exhibiting the behavior that corresponds to humility?

In regard to our conduct toward God, humility disposes us:

- to freely and heartily admit our smallness. It is a delight to a humble soul to confess his unworthiness.

- to distrust self, and depend only on God. The proud love their self-sufficiency, but the humble love to cast themselves on God for refuge.

- to renounce the honor for any good we do, and give it all to God, who alone is truly worthy. "Not unto us, O Lord, not unto us, but unto thy name give glory, for thy mercy, and for thy truth's sake" (Ps. 115:1).

- to fully submit ourselves to God. Seeing we are so inferior to Him, it is only proper that He rule over us. We are at His disposal every day. The worst we receive from His hand is better than we deserve. "Though he slay me, yet will I trust in him" (Job 13:15).

In regard to our conduct toward men, humility tends to prevent:

- an aspiring and ambitious behavior. Humility brings contentment with our lot. We "mind not high things" (Rom. 12:16).

– an ostentatious behavior. If we have any advantages, we will not be showy and flamboyant with them. We will not parade our superior gifts or experiences. Pride causes a Pharisee to do all his works to be seen of men (Matt. 23:5). But humility says, "It is a very small thing that I should be judged of you" (1 Cor. 4:3).

– an arrogant and assuming behavior. We will not expect others to treat us as superior. Rather we will give place to others. "In lowliness of mind," we will "esteem others better" than ourselves, since we are "less than the least of all saints" (Phil. 2:3; Eph. 3:8).

– scornful behavior. What could be more offensive than to treat others with sneering contempt and *vaunting* of self? There are many ways to enlarge ourselves by belittling others. But humility enables us to "condescend to men of low estate" (Rom. 12:16), no matter how great we seem to be.

– willful and stubborn behavior. We will not always insist on our will or our plan. Humility leads us to yield to others for the sake of peace, as long as we are not violating truth and holiness. The principle here is stated in these questions from 1 Corinthians 6:7, "Why do ye not rather take wrong? why do ye not rather suffer yourselves to be defrauded?"

– leveling behavior, that is, insisting on bringing down those that are above us. Instead, we understand that God has ordained various ranks in society, and we are willing to "render therefore to all their dues: tribute to whom tribute is due; custom to whom custom; fear to whom fear; honour to whom honour" (Rom. 13:7).

– self-justifying behavior. Rather, we will readily acknowledge our faults with shame. What but pride keeps us from "confessing our faults one to another" (James 5:16), or from receiving a rebuke thankfully? "Let the righteous smite me; it shall be a kindness" (Ps. 141:5).

II. How the spirit of love is a humble spirit

1. Love implies and tends to humility.

Love implies humility in that true Christian love is a humble love. Love that is not humble is a forgery. As we observed earlier, it is especially a sight of the loveliness of God that melts a soul in utter humiliation before Him. We must have an appreciation not only for His greatness, but also for His goodness. Without the latter, we may be convinced of our danger before God, but we will not be convicted of our offensiveness to God. Lost men and angels may sense the wide distance between themselves and God, but they are not humbled thereby. But as we sense His loveliness, we cannot but be humbled with respect to God and man.

Love implies humility in that, when God is truly loved, He is loved as an infinite superior. We cannot love Him as an equal; we must love Him with a humble love as one inferior to Him.

Love tends to humility. Humility is not only a quality inherent in love, but is also an effect of love. Love inclines the heart to the spirit and behavior that is befitting the distance from the beloved one. Those whom we love, we are willing to honor above ourselves. Fallen creatures refuse to honor God, and they despise the distance between themselves and God. But when Christian love enters a heart, we are inclined to the humble respect that befits the distance between God and us. Likewise, love to man, arising from love to God, tends to humble behavior in our relationships with our neighbors.

Furthermore, love to God tends to a hating of sin against Him. To the extent that we love anything, in like measure we will hate that which is contrary to it. If we love God, we must abhor sin, and abhor ourselves for our sin. Thus, we will humble ourselves before our great and holy God.

2. The gospel tends to draw forth such exercises of love as do especially imply and tend to humility.

The gospel leads us to love God as an infinitely condescending God. How far He has stooped to take a gracious notice of poor, vile worms of the dust, and to send His precious Son to die for us, that we might be forgiven and honored and enjoy Him forever! The most fitting response from us to such infinite condescension is utter humility.

The gospel leads us to love Christ as a humble Person. Seeing He is both God and man, He has not only condescension but also humility, the like of which has never existed in any other. He is "meek and lowly in heart" (Matt. 11:29). "He humbled himself, and became obedient unto death" (Phil. 2:8). Since He is a humble Master to us, we must humble ourselves before Him, lest the servant be above his lord (Matt. 10:24). He who bent down to wash the feet of His disciples tells us, "Whosoever will be great among you, let him be your minister; and whosoever will be chief among you, let him be your servant: even as the Son of man came not to be ministered unto, but to minister, and to give his life a ransom for many" (Matt. 20:26–28).

The gospel leads us to love Christ as a crucified Savior. Though He was the Lord of glory, He suffered the greatest reproach and ignominy in His death. What should this truth kindle in our hearts, more than a spirit of humility and a pouring of contempt on all our pride. If we profess to be the followers of the meek and lowly One, we shall walk humbly before God and man all the days of our life.

The gospel leads us to love Christ as One crucified for our sakes. His death for our sins should cause us to hate our sins exceedingly, to love Him supremely, and to take a very humble stance before Him. What greater inducement to humility could we have? In His cross-bearing for our sakes, we see cause for humility because of our sinfulness and His loveliness.

Let us make some applications.

1. Consider the excellence of a Christian spirit.

Much of the excellence of the righteous consists in their Christ-like humility. It is spoken of as a rich jewel, "the ornament of a meek and quiet spirit, which is in the sight of God of great price" (1 Peter 3:4).

2. Examine whether your spirit be truly humble.

There are many counterfeits. For example:

– Some pretend to be humble.

– Some are naturally quiet or lack a strong personality.

– Some tend to despondency.

– Some are briefly convicted over some specific sin.

– Some are abased while in affliction.

– Some are simply deceived by Satan.

Therefore, make sure that your humility is of the genuine sort, as taught and exhibited in the gospel, and taught by the Holy Spirit. This is a vital concern, for "God resisteth the proud, but giveth grace unto the humble" (James 4:6).

3. Let those who are strangers to saving grace seek the Savior, so that they might attain this excellent spirit of humility.

Outside of Christ, you are proud against God, and utterly destitute of any real humility, no matter how meek and humble you appear in the eyes of men. You live in rebellion against God, who demands and deserves your humility. You refuse to comply with the humbling conditions and way of salvation by Christ Jesus. Remember that such a proud spirit is characteristic of devils. "Not a novice, lest being lifted up with pride he fall into the condemnation of the devil" (1 Tim. 3:6). The book of Proverbs is full of warnings against the proud. "Every one that is proud in heart is an abomination to the LORD: though hand join in hand, he shall not be unpunished" (16:5). Look at Pharaoh, Korah, Haman, Belshazzaar, and Herod, and consider where your pride will lead. Learn from these examples to cherish humility and to walk humbly with thy God. Look to Christ for redemption from the sin of pride.

4. Let us all seek more of a humble spirit, endeavoring to be humble in all our dealings with God and man.

Know God. Confess your nothingness before Him. Know yourself. Confess your pride against God. Distrust yourself, and rely only on Him. Renounce all glory except from Him. Yield yourself to His will. Avoid all proud behavior. Seek and strive after the humble spirit manifested by Christ in His life on this earth. Prize the grace of humility as God in His Word prizes it. It is the spirit with which He will dwell on earth, as well as in heaven. "For thus saith the high and lofty One that inhabiteth eternity, whose name is Holy; I dwell in the high and holy place, with him also that is of a contrite and humble spirit, to revive the spirit of the humble, and to revive the heart of the contrite ones" (Isa. 57:15).

8

LOVE IS OPPOSITE OF A SELFISH SPIRIT

Charity . . . seeketh not her own.
— 1 Corinthians 13:5

The fall of man into sin consisted in part in his losing the higher benevolent principles of his nature and descending into inordinate self-love. Before the fall, his nature reflected the very nature of God, in that he was mindful of others and their welfare. He was especially mindful of God Himself. But after the fall, self-love became the absolute master of his soul. Sin, like a powerful astringent, restricted and confined his soul to small dimensions of selfishness. Yet God, in redemption through Jesus Christ, restores the enlargement of heart in man, and liberates him to once again embrace his fellow-creatures and to be swallowed up in love to his Creator. The doctrine of the text before us is, *the spirit of charity or Christian love is opposite of a selfish spirit.*

I. The nature of selfishness

Not all self-love is sin. It is good that a person should love his own happiness. Without this, he ceases to be a man altogether. If we did not love our happiness, it would not be happiness to us at all. The command to love our neighbor as ourselves (Matt. 19:19), presup-

47

poses that we may, and must, love ourselves. We are not command-ed to love our neighbor *more* than ourselves, but *as* ourselves. And since our love to our neighbor is next to our love to God, we are therefore to love ourselves next to God. The threats and promises of Scripture all appeal to our natural and proper self-love, either in fears of misery or hopes of happiness.

The self-love that love opposes is a sinful, inordinate self-love. Since this is an easily misunderstood matter, we must think and speak clearly concerning it.

Negatively, inordinate self-love does not consist in the degree in which a person loves himself and his happiness. Proper self-love does not admit of increase or decrease. In conversion, God does gives us a new happiness, but He does not remove from us any love of happiness. In sanctification, love for happiness is not diminished, but rather it is regulated as to its exercises, influence, and the courses and objects to which it leads. In glorification, if our love of happiness were to diminish, so would our love of holiness, for holiness is happiness.

Positively, an inordinate self-love consists in one of two things. First, it may be too great comparatively. Man's proper self-love turned into inordinate self-love when his love for God and for his fellow-man disappeared in the fall. It was not that his self-love increased, but that his love for others vanished, and thus the comparative size of self-love increased. In one sense, sinners do not love themselves enough; they do not love their own soul's happiness as they should. Therefore, we read, "He that refuseth instruction despiseth his own soul, and Whoso is partner with a thief hateth his own soul" (Prov. 15:32; 29:24). In one sense he hates himself, though in another sense he loves himself too much.

Second, self-love is inordinate when a man places his happiness in that which is confined to himself. He directs his self-love in the wrong channel. His is a love that "seeketh her own," that is, one that seeks her own private good, a good limited to self, a good that excludes others. It is this sinful self-appropriating love of which we read in Philippians 2:21, "All seek their own, not the things which are Jesus Christ's." Paul warns against those who are "lovers of their own selves," which must be understood as inordinate self-love (2 Tim. 3:2).

Let us not fail to distinguish clearly between a sinful and a proper self-love. If the happiness we long for is to enjoy God, behold His glory, and hold communion with Him, then loving God is the same act as loving ourselves. Furthermore, as a Christian longs for the happiness of his fellow-man, he enlarges his own happiness as he enlarges that of the other. But this is far from sinful self-love.

II. How the spirit of love is contrary to a selfish spirit

It leads us to seek not only our own things, but also the things of others. Such a spirit seeks to please and glorify God. It "seeks the things which are Jesus Christ's" (Phil. 2:21). Christ is the great end of our life. "For me to live is Christ" (Phil. 1:21). We are servants of God, "doing His will from the heart" (Eph. 6:6). Eating, drinking, and all our doing, we do "to the glory of God" (1 Cor. 10:31).

Such a spirit seeks the good of our fellow-creatures. "Look not every man on his own things, but every man also on the things of others" (Phil. 2:4). Their spiritual happiness should be our special interest. Also, their temporal prosperity should concern us.

Such a spirit sympathizes with the difficulties, burdens, and afflictions of others. A selfish heart thinks only of its own misery. But a truly loving heart is filled with mercy for the miseries of others, and is ready to help, supply, and relieve.

Such a spirit is liberal, ready to assist the needs of others, as there may be opportunity. "As we have therefore opportunity, let us do good unto all men, especially unto them who are of the household of faith" (Gal. 6:10).

Such a spirit in a man makes him conscious of his obligation to the community around him. He will endeavor to promote the welfare of his city and his nation. He will be concerned about the spiritual benefit he might give to others, especially those of his own church. Those who occupy positions of leadership, whether in government or in church, will be disposed by the spirit of love to serve the highest interests of those under their care. Whereas the selfish person is like sinning Israel who "were not grieved for the affliction of Joseph," the charitable person, like David, is remembered as one who "served his own generation by the will of God" (Amos 6:6; Acts 13:36).

The spirit of love disposes us in many cases to part with our own things for the sake of others. We will forego our own private interest for the good of our neighbors. Not only our possessions, but also our very lives we count not dear unto ourselves (Acts 20:24). "We ought to lay down our lives for the brethren" (1 John 3:16).

III. Evidence that supports the principle of the selflessness of love

The nature of love in general. It is the very nature of love to be diffusive, to espouse the interests of others. Selfishness contracts the heart, but love enlarges it and makes it extend to others, as if they had become part of the man himself. If they are injured, he is injured; if they are promoted, he is promoted.

The peculiar nature of Christian or divine love. Christian love is the only love that operates on a principle higher than that of selfishness. An unregenerate heart can love others, as long as they in some way promote his self-interest. Such a love is purely natural. But the love of our text is supernatural. It is a gift from God that rises above self and self-interest. Natural love may appear generous and opposed to selfishness, but ultimately it agrees with a selfish spirit because it springs from a principle of self-love. However, the Christian's love to his fellow-man springs from a principle of divine love. He loves others because he loves God who made them. This enables him to love even his enemies. No natural love can do this.

The nature of Christian love to God and man. As for love to God, the first and great commandment instructs us of the nature of this love. It is a love that devotes all of itself to God without reservation, with all the heart, soul, mind and strength (Mark 12:30). But a selfish heart never devotes itself to another; rather it expects others to devote themselves to it. Thus, self becomes god.

As for love to man, we are taught in the Old Testament to love our neighbor as ourselves (Lev. 19:18). In the New Testament, we are given a new commandment: "A new commandment I give unto you, That ye love one another; as I have loved you, that ye also love one another" (John 13:34). The newness of this command is not found in the duty to love others, which was already in place, but in the rule and motive annexed to it, which we see so clearly in the gospel. Christ's love is now our pattern, not just our love for self. As we consider the supreme example of Christ as an enforcement to self-denying love, let us mark four points.

First, Christ loved those who were His enemies. We were not merely lacking in love to Him; we were full of enmity and actual hatred against Him. "But God commendeth his love toward us, in that, while we were yet sinners, Christ died for us. . . . [W]hen we were enemies, we were reconciled to God by the death of his Son" (Rom. 5:8, 10).

Second, Christ's love is such a love that in some respects He looked on us as Himself. He made our interest His interest, even to the point of making our sin His sin. He assumed our guilt, so that it might be looked upon as His own, while imputing to us His righteousness, so that it might be looked upon as our own.

Third, Christ spent Himself for our sakes. His love was not in mere word or feeling, but in deed and in truth. His sacrifices were not small, but so great as to give up His own ease, comfort, interest, honor, and wealth. He became poor, despised, and had no place to lay His head. But even more, He shed His blood and laid down His life, offering Himself a sacrifice to God in our behalf, that we might be forgiven, accepted, and saved!

Fourth, Christ loved us without any expectation of ever being repaid by us for His love. He knew we were poor, miserable, empty-handed outcasts who could render nothing to Him in return for His love. He knew that whatever He gave must be given freely, or it could not be given at all. His love to us did not depend on our love to Him.

If such an example of love inflames our hearts, we will likewise love the unlovely freely and be willing to hazard ourselves without reservation for their good. We cannot follow Christ and remain selfish.

The great application of this text is that we should turn away from a selfish spirit, and live a life that is contrary to it. We should seek to be devoted to God first, and then to our neighbor. To stir us up to this action, let us consider the following.

1. You do not belong to yourself.

Man is not made by himself, nor is he made for himself. There is a higher authority, a higher end. God made you for Himself. He has placed high and noble ends before you: to serve Him and your fellow-man. As a Christian, you are not your own, but you have been bought with a very precious price, the blood of Christ (1 Cor. 6:19, 20; 1 Peter 1:19). If you treat yourself as your own, you are guilty of robbing Christ who purchased you. All you have belongs to Him and is at His disposal. He is the Master; you are the steward.

2. You are united to Christ and to your fellow-Christians.

The apostle uses the illustration of our body to teach us about our duty to one another. No part of our body is self-serving. Rather, each part serves the others and promotes the common good of the whole. If one part is wounded or suffers, all the other parts become engaged in protecting and attending to it. Even the ears help the other organs by listening to the instructions of the physician! In Christ's spiritual body, the same care should be manifested, so that in all things Christ, who is our head, might be glorified.

3. As you seek the glory of God and the good of others, you will find that God will seek your interests and promote your welfare.

Here is a great truth. No matter how much you deny yourself for God's sake, you will not throw yourself away. God will take care of you. He will see to it that your sacrifices are not in vain. Though He will never be a debtor to man, He does freely repay all that you spend for Him. He promised, "There is no man that hath left house, or brethren, or sisters, or father, or mother, or wife, or children, or lands, for my sake, and the gospel's, but he shall receive an hundredfold now in this time, houses, and brethren, and sisters, and mothers, and children, and lands, with persecutions; and in the world to come eternal life" (Mark 10:29–30). When we consider the infinite and indescribable bliss of eternity, we discover that He more than repays all that we selflessly give!

God has arranged things in such a way that not to seek your own in the selfish sense, is the best way to seek your own in a better sense. If you love God and serve others, you will in the long run promote your own highest interests. You will find true pleasure here below and a crown of glory with pleasures forever at God's right hand. All things will be yours, even God Himself (1 Cor. 3:21– 22).

But if you selfishly seek your own, God will leave you to yourself, to promote your interests as best you can. If you seek to grasp all as your own, you will lose it and will at last be driven out of the world to everlasting poverty and contempt. Therefore, let us strive by God's grace to overcome our selfishness and have the spirit that *seeketh not her own.*

9

LOVE IS OPPOSITE OF AN ANGRY SPIRIT

Charity . . . is not easily provoked.
— 1 Corinthians 13:5

Having considered that love is contrary to the two great evils of pride and selfishness, we now consider some of the common fruits of these evils. The phrase before us expresses that *the spirit of charity or Christian love is the opposite of an angry, wrathful disposition.*

I. A spirit of anger defined

Not all anger is evil. Believers are exhorted, "Be ye angry" (Eph. 4:26). It is possible to be angry on some occasions without offending God. When is anger a sin? Let us mark four instances when it may be undue and unsuitable to be angry.

Anger may be a sin with respect to its nature. We must carefully distinguish between sinful anger and mere opposition of the mind, in cool judgment, against someone or something perceived to be evil. We must also distinguish opposition of one's spirit against natural evil such as grief and sorrow, which is not sinful anger. We must further distinguish opposition against moral evil in voluntary agents and disapproval of those moral agents themselves, neither of which is sinful anger. There may be a dislike without the spirit becoming excited and angry. In all anger there must be a moving of the feelings or emotions or affections of man. Anger is an earnest passion in the soul that opposes real or imaginary evil.

This passion becomes an evil affection when it contains ill will or a desire for personal revenge. Christians are required to wish well to all, to pray for all, and even to bless those that persecute them (Matt. 5:44). "Bless and curse not," we are instructed (Rom. 12:14). Of course, the vengeance that public justice executes against evildoers is not forbidden, seeing the magistrate acts not for himself but for God. But personal ill will and revenge is always forbidden. "Thou shalt not avenge, nor bear any grudge against the children of thy people; but thou shalt love thy neighbor as thyself" (Lev. 19:18). "Avenge not yourselves, but rather give place unto wrath: for it is written, Vengeance is mine; I will repay, saith the Lord" (Rom. 12:19). All anger of this kind is strictly prohibited in Scripture. "Let all bitterness, and wrath, and anger, and clamor, and evil-speaking, be put away from you, with all malice" (Eph. 4:31).

Anger may be a sin with respect to its occasion. If there is no just cause, then it is sin. "Whosoever is angry with his brother without a cause shall be in danger of the judgment" (Matt. 5:22). Let us consider when there is no just cause for anger.

First, there is no just cause for anger when there is no fault in the person who is the object of the anger. Many people vent their sinful anger against those who had nothing to do with the matter in the first place, or else did the best they could in the matter. Sometimes anger is directed against those who did good, for which they ought to be praised. All such anger is ultimately directed against God and His providence. The prophet Jonah became angry with God's sparing Nineveh, and even defended his sinful passion. God asked Jonah, "Doest thou well to be angry?" And Jonah answered, "I do well to be angry" (Jonah 4:9). If we are angry at any of God's providences, we are truly angry at God Himself, the Author of providence. Furthermore, how many saints have suffered simply because they were saints? Their holy life, their good deeds, their loving rebuke, their enforcing of the church covenant, were the occasions of their being hated. Thus, they entered into the sufferings of Christ, whom the priests and Pharisees "hated without a cause" (John 15:25).

Second, there is no just cause for anger when a person is angry over small, trivial matters. Some people become stirred to anger by every little thing in others – in family, in society, in business – which are no greater faults than they themselves are guilty of every day. Such a soul will be continually angry in this fallen, cursed world in which we live. "He that is soon angry dealeth foolishly" (Prov. 14:17). A charitable man will be slow to anger, and he will become provoked only on unusual occasions that demand godly anger.

Third, there is no just cause for anger when our feelings and emotions are stirred at the faults of others because they are against us, and not because they are against God. We should never be angry, except at sin, and then only as it is sin against God. We sin in our anger when we are selfish in it. Our anger should be like Christ's. Under the greatest of personal injuries, He was like a lamb. His only occasions of anger occurred when defending the cause of His Father against sin.

Anger may be a sin with respect to its end. Reason must have a hand in the matter, as we consider the proper end, advantage and benefit that our anger will gain toward those concerned. God's glory should be our great aim. Otherwise, our anger is simply the blind passion of beasts. We must be guided in all things by biblically-governed reason. If any wrong end is in view, such as the gratification of our own pride, then our anger is sinful.

Anger may be a sin with respect to its measure. This may be considered in two aspects.

First, anger is a sin when it is immoderate in its degree. The degree of the anger should never exceed what is required to gain the good ends which reason has proposed. We must never lose control, as if we were drunk on our passions and beside ourselves.

Second, anger is sin when it is immoderate in its continuance. Scripture commands, "Be ye angry, and sin not: let not the sun go down upon your wrath" (Eph. 4:26), giving us to know that even righteous anger must be short-lived. Otherwise it becomes a simmering grudge that lasts for days or perhaps years. This encourages an attitude of hatred, and is a great sin in God's sight.

II. How a Christian spirit is contrary to a spirit of anger

Christian love is in itself contrary to all undue anger. The nature of love is goodwill, not ill will. It is backward to anger and revenge. Christian love is slow to take personal offense, and is concerned with offenses inasmuch as they are against God.

All the fruits of Christian love mentioned in the context are contrary to all undue anger. We will only mention the two great fruits that we have considered thus far, as they stand for all other virtues.

First, love is humble; it opposes pride. Yet pride is one of the great causes of undue anger. An elevated sense of self-importance leads a man to be unreasonable and rash in his anger.

Second, love is generous; it opposes selfishness. Yet seeking our own interests first is another great cause of hasty, inconsiderate, immoderate and long-continued wrath. Men who seek their own glory are easily provoked.

Let us now endeavor to apply this truth to our own hearts.

1. Let us examine ourselves.

Does your conscience speak to you now? How often have you been angry? And how often was it without a just cause? Do you justify your anger by saying it is for God's cause, when in reality it is only your private interest that was affected? Are you slow to anger and of little zeal when only God's interest is affected?

What good has been obtained by your anger; what was your aim in it? How many times has the sun set on your anger while God and your neighbor knew about it? Are you even now sitting before

God with anger laid up and burning in your heart? Or is it like a smothered fire in the heaps of autumn leaves, which the least breeze will kindle into a flame? In your family relations, have you been a source of discord? Have you stirred yourself to anger when the occasion was a small trifling fault in another, or perhaps you were partly to blame?

Let us examine ourselves to know what manner of spirit we are of.

2. Let us avoid all undue and sinful anger.

The heart of man is so prone to anger by its natural pride and selfishness, and the world is so full of occasions to stir up this corruption with us, that if we are to live as a Christian should, we must constantly watch and pray. We must fight not only against the outbreak of sinful anger, but we must also fight against and mortify the very principle of anger, establishing and increasing in love. To this end, let us mention four things to consider.

First, consider your own failings, by which you have given God and man occasion to be justly angry with you. All your life you have come short of God's requirements. You rightly deserve His wrath, yet you ask Him for mercy. Likewise, you expect your fellow-man to pardon you. Therefore, before you become angry with others, reflect upon your own errors and see if you have not done as much as or worse than others.

Second, consider how your undue anger destroys your own comfort. You starve your own peace and happiness while feeding your own restlessness and misery.

Third, consider how an angry spirit makes you unfit for religious duties. Our Lord taught us not to approach His altar while we are at enmity with others, but "first be reconciled to thy brother, and then come and offer thy gift" (Matt. 5:24). Men are to "pray every where, lifting up holy hands, without wrath and doubting" (1 Tim. 2:8).

Fourth, consider that sinful anger makes you unfit for human society. We are expressly taught this in Proverbs 22:24, "Make no friendship with an angry man; and with a furious man thou shalt not go." It leaves you a troublemaker and a pest of society. "An angry man stirreth up strife" (Prov. 29:22). It leaves you disapproved by God and man, and makes you more fit for hell than for heaven. Therefore, let us cultivate a gentle, kind spirit, which is the spirit of love and of heaven.

10

LOVE IS OPPOSITE OF A CRITICAL SPIRIT

Charity . . . thinketh no evil.
— 1 Corinthians 13:5

Another common fruit of pride and selfishness is a critical spirit. Therefore, *love is contrary to a critical, judgmental, censorious spirit.* Christian love enables us to think the best of others that their case will allow.

I. A critical spirit defined

A critical spirit appears in an inclination to judge evil concerning others. It is true that some people are quick to judge favorably when they see a little good in others. But some are quick to judge unfavorably when they see a little evil in others. All certainty in such matters belongs to God alone, who is the Searcher of men's hearts.

We are guilty of this sin when we condemn others for things that do not evidence a bad state. Job's friends misread Providence and wrongly judged his case. We are guilty of this sin when we condemn others for the failings that all of God's children commit (which are sometimes less than what we ourselves have committed). We are guilty of this sin when we condemn as unregenerate those who differ from us on some secondary point, or those whose temperament or outward advantages are not just like our own. We should not set up ourselves and our experience as the standard for all others. The Spirit of God is at liberty to work in a variety of ways.

A critical spirit appears in an inclination to judge as evil the qualities of others. We manifest this spirit when we overlook the good qualities of others and magnify their bad qualities. Some are ready to charge others with ignorance and folly when they do not deserve it. Some are ready to charge others with immorality when they are not at all guilty, or are guilty in a smaller degree. Some are so prejudiced against their neighbors that they think them purely proud, selfish, spiteful, and malicious, when in fact they have many good qualities evident to everyone else. But the uncharitable soul is always looking for evil.

A critical spirit appears in an inclination to judge as evil the actions of others as to their words or deeds.

First, this spirit condemns them without any compelling evidence that requires such a judgment. A censorious person makes his judgments based on what he supposes, not on what he sees and knows. He is guilty of "evil surmisings" (1 Tim. 6:4). He is ready to take up and circulate evil reports about others, rather than to question them or find out the truth. Like his father, the devil, he is a liar! "A liar giveth ear to a naughty tongue" (Prov. 17:4). The gossiper finds pleasure in hearing evil about others. He feeds on it like a vulture on carrion. But a charitable spirit "taketh not up a reproach against his neighbor" (Ps. 15:3).

Second, a critical disposition is ready to put the worst construction on the actions of others. This spirit is far too common. The uncharitable person quickly assumes the good actions of others to be hypocrisy. He is suspicious of any show of concern for public good, or good of a neighbor, or the honor of God. In reality, he himself is the hypocrite who entertains this evil design in his heart.

Perhaps you ask, *Is there not a place for some judgment? Is not some criticism lawful?* I will answer in two parts.

First, God has appointed public judges in society, both in civil government and in church government, who must impartially judge according to the evidence, as to its agreement or disagreement with the law.

Second, no private person is obligated to divest himself of reason in order that he may judge favorably concerning everyone. Christian love is not founded on the ruins of reason! Rather, love and reason enjoy a sweet harmony. It is no sin to judge others who give plain and clear evidence of evil doing. It is not sin to judge as unregenerate those who give flagrant proof of it. "Some men's sins are open beforehand, going before to judgment; and some men they follow after" (1 Tim. 5:24).

The sin of being judgmental lies in one of two things.

First, it lies in judging evil of others when evidence does not obligate us to it, or when the case very well allows us to think well of others. As we have said, we must not overlook that which is favorable to their case, nor magnify that which is against it. Love obliges us to suspend our judgment until we know more of the matter. "He that answereth a matter before he heareth it, it is folly and shame unto him" (Prov. 18:13).

Second, the sin of being judgmental lies in the enjoyment of judging ill of others. A father who sees compelling evidence against his child must condemn him, but he does so with great grief. But if a person loves to think the worst of others and finds pleasure in judging them, he is a stranger to the spirit of love. If we have a spirit of love, we will be cautious in passing judgment, doing so only when the nature of the case warrants, and after we have put the best construction on the words and actions of others. When we are obligated, against our inclination, to think evil of another, we will be hesitant to tell others about it, and will only do so when a sense of duty requires us.

II. A critical spirit is contrary to a Christian spirit

It is contrary to love toward our neighbor. We are naturally reluctant to judge evil in ourselves, because we love ourselves. So, if we love others as ourselves, we will also be reluctant to judge evil in them. Furthermore, we are reluctant to judge evil of anyone that we love, such as family and friends. This spirit of love should extend to all men. But where hatred and ill will prevails toward others, a critical spirit prevails also. When two people or parties have a falling out, they are always ready to judge the worst of each other. One of the first things the critical spirit says is, "My enemy is not a Christian."

A critical spirit manifests a proud spirit. The critical person imagines himself to be free from the faults and blemishes that he condemns in others. If we were humbly conscious of our own failings, we would be slow to judge others. The same kind of corruptions dwell in one heart as in another. "Therefore thou art inexcusable, O man, whosoever thou art that judgest: for wherein thou judgest another, thou condemnest thyself; for thou that judgest doest the same things" (Rom. 2:1). If we examine our own hearts as carefully as others, we will find as much cause for censure in ourselves as in them. The one who judges sets himself up above others, even as if he were above the law itself. "He that speaketh evil of his brother, and judgeth his brother, speaketh evil of the law, and judgeth the law: but if thou judge the law, thou art not a doer of the law, but a judge" (James 4:11). What arrogance and pride!

What should we learn from this?

1. This principle reproves those who commonly speak evil of others.

If thinking evil concerning someone is much to be condemned, how much more is evil speaking condemned? Untold damage is done by uncharitable, backbiting tongues, and Scripture roundly forbids such. Titus was instructed by Paul to remind the believers "to speak evil of no man, to be no brawlers, but gentle, showing all meekness unto all men" (Titus 3:2). Have you not often been guilty of this sin of evil speaking, especially against those with whom you had some difficulty, or who are of a different party than yourself? Do you not allow yourself to practice this evil day by day? Such a spirit is contrary to true Christianity and must be forsaken at once.

2. This principle warns us against all manner of wrong criticism in thought or word.

Consider how often, when the truth comes out, things appear more favorable toward others than we had at first thought. For example, Eli thought that Hannah was drunk, but in fact she was a sober woman agonizing in prayer. Elijah imagined himself to be the one and only true follower of Jehovah, but God had reserved seven thousand faithful souls. There are always two sides to every story, and it is generally wise and safe and charitable to believe the best side. Never presume the worst. Wait until all the truth is revealed.

Consider how little occasion there is for us to pass sentence on others. Our great concern is with ourselves, not others. Even if others deserve our censure, it pertains to God's jurisdiction more than ours. We ought not to take a work upon us which is rightfully His. He has appointed a day for His decision. "Therefore judge nothing before the time, until the Lord come, who both will bring to light the hidden things of darkness, and will make manifest the counsels of the hearts: and then shall every man have praise of God" (1 Cor. 4:5).

Consider that God has threatened that if we wrongfully judge others, we ourselves will be judged. "Judge not, that ye be not judged." For with what judgment ye judge, ye shall be judged (Matt. 7:1–2). "And thinkest thou this, O man, that judgest them which do such things, and doest the same, that thou shalt escape the judgment of God?" (Rom. 2:3). Our great concern is to be acquitted by our Judge at the last day. Therefore, if we would not receive a just condemnation from Him, let us not unjustly condemn others.

11

ALL TRUE GRACE IN THE HEART TENDS TO HOLY PRACTICE IN THE LIFE

Charity . . . rejoiceth not in iniquity, but rejoiceth in the truth.
— 1 Corinthians 13:6

With these words, the apostle sums up all good tendencies of love in respect to active conduct. It is as if he says, "I need not multiply particular instances. In a word, love is contrary to everything in life and practice that is evil and promotes everything that is good."

The term *iniquity* speaks of everything that is sinful in the life and practice. The term *truth* speaks of everything good and virtuous and holy. *Truth* in this context includes both the knowledge of truth and conformity to it.

The great doctrine here is that *all true Christian grace in the heart tends to holy practice in the life.* If any man thinks that grace in the heart may lie dormant and not control the direction in which a person goes, he entertains a very wrong notion of the Christian life. Our text expresses, in both negative and positive terms, that grace in the heart cannot but operate in the whole life.

I. Arguments in support of this doctrine

Holiness of life is the great end of our election by God, which is the first

67

ground of all grace. Contrary to what many think, holy practice is not the ground and reason of election, but rather holy practice is the aim and end of election. God did not choose men because He saw in advance that they would be holy, but He chose men so that He might make them holy. Our Lord said, "Ye have not chosen me, but I have chosen you, and ordained you, that ye should go and bring forth fruit, and that your fruit should remain" (John 15:16). Ephesians 2:10 tells us that God has appointed beforehand the holy works of His people. "We are his workmanship, created in Christ Jesus unto good works, which God hath before ordained that we should walk in them."

Holiness of life is the great end of redemption. Christ's mission from heaven to earth was to "save his people from their sins" (Matt. 1:21). Shortly before His death, He prayed, "For their sakes I sanctify myself, that they also might be sanctified through the truth" (John 17:19). Paul explains to Titus that the whole purpose of Christ's "giving himself for us was that he might redeem us from all iniquity, and purify unto himself a peculiar people, zealous of good works" (2:14). This truth was typified in the demand repeatedly made to Pharaoh, "Let my people go, that they may serve me" (Ex. 7:16, etc.)

Holiness of life is the great end of effectual calling or saving conversion. "For God hath not called us unto uncleanness, but unto holiness" (1 Thess. 4:7). "As he which hath called you is holy, so be ye holy in all manner of conversation" (1 Peter 1:15).

Holiness of life is the tendency of true spiritual knowledge and understanding. There is, of course, such a thing as speculative knowledge, which many wicked men have attained in a high measure. They may reason strongly about the attributes of God and the doctrines of Christianity. But there is an eternity of difference between such speculative knowledge and true practical knowledge. He who truly knows God, sees the hatefulness of sin and the beauty of holiness. This knowledge tends to incline him to walk in ways of holiness. He knows that God is worthy of his obedience.

A lack of this knowledge kept Pharaoh from obeying God. "Who is the LORD, that I should obey his voice to let Israel go? I know not the LORD, neither will I let Israel go" (Ex. 5:2). The Psalmist asks, "Have all the workers of iniquity no knowledge? who eat up my people as they eat bread, and call not upon the LORD" (Ps. 14:4). According to Jeremiah 22:16, the knowledge of God leads to holy behavior: "He judged the cause of the poor and needy; then it was well with him: was not this to know me? saith the LORD." We see the same connection in 1 John 2:4, "He that saith, I know him, and keepeth not his commandments, is a liar, and the truth is not in him."

Consider some arguments from the very principle of grace itself:

First, the immediate seat of grace is in the will or disposition. This faculty commands all our actions. When we speak of a man's practice, we speak of those things he does as a free and voluntary agent. All his executive powers are subject to the faculty of the will. Therefore, if grace be in our will, it must necessarily lead to gracious practice.

Second, the very definition of grace is that it is a principle of holy action. A principle of grace has as much relation to practice as a root has to the plant. It is as absurd to speak of a root without the plant as to speak of a principle of grace that does not tend to the practice of grace.

Third, that which is real can be distinguished from that which is only a shadow by effectual operations. A picture of a man may look very real and powerful, but it cannot act. Likewise, grace that is merely in appearance does not act, but grace that is real brings to pass actions of holiness.

Fourth, in the Scriptures, natural man is described as spiritually dead, without holy principles or actions, bringing nothing to pass that is truly good. But the regenerate are described as alive, and therefore, moving and walking and filling their days with works that demonstrate the existence of life.

Fifth, Christian grace is not only a principle of life, but also an exceedingly powerful principle. The power at work in the children of God is nothing less than the mighty power that raised up Christ from the grave (Eph. 1:19–20).

II. Further proof of this doctrine

Other graces demonstrate the connection between a good heart and a holy life.

The grace of faith in Jesus Christ tends to holy practice. True faith is the kind "that worketh by love" (Gal. 5:6). James chapter two teaches us that faith is demonstrated by our works. If a man really believes a report, he will act upon it. If he does not believe it to be true, he will act as though he never heard it. Our practice is according to our convictions. Faith leads us to forego other ways of securing happiness because we are convinced that Christ alone is sufficient to bestow happiness. Also, faith leads us not only to a Savior from the punishment of sin, but also from sin itself. The man who has not willed that sin and he should part, cannot have willed to receive Christ as his Savior to part them. In other words, Christ does not become a man's Savior unless He also becomes His Lord. The priestly office of Christ cannot be divided from His kingly office. Furthermore, if we are genuinely trusting Christ, we will trust Him with everything. We will venture all on Him, and be willing to undergo all labor, watching, warfare, and suffering, knowing that He will more than make up for whatever losses we sustain.

The grace of love to God tends to holy practice. Love of some kind or other influences all our life and actions. If a man loves money, he pursues money with his actions. If he loves honor, or carnal pleasure, he pursues those things; his life is regulated by them. Even so, if a man loves God, his practice will be regulated by it. Our actions are the truest test of our affections. If a man says he loves his friend but never labors nor suffers for him, his words are vain. Real love evidences itself in fruits of conduct. Love to God is exercised in highly esteeming Him, choosing Him, desiring Him, delighting in Him. If our honor or money or ease compete with God, we must cleave to God and let these other things go. We prove the sincerity of our love to Him by our obedience to Him. If we give up one thing for the sake of another, we demonstrate that we were not fully satisfied with the first thing.

The grace of repentance tends to holy practice. Repentance is a change of mind with respect to sin and righteousness and God. True turning from sin cannot remain purely in the mind; it will show itself in a change of conduct. The man will forsake sin and avoid it. If he goes on in it just as he did before, there is no reason to believe he heartily repented of it.

The grace of humility tends to holy practice. He that is conscious of his own littleness, nothingness, and unworthiness will carry himself accordingly before God and man. Humility of heart has as strong a tendency to influence our practice as does pride of heart. If we are humble, we will practice patience, submission, and reverence toward God. Toward man we will be meek, courteous, respectful, gentle, peaceful, easily entreated, content, quiet, ready to forgive, not self-willed, not envious.

The grace of the fear of God tends to holy practice. The main idea in fearing God is that we dread offending Him by sinning against Him. "The fear of the LORD is to hate evil" (Prov. 8:13). The fear of God is often spoken of in connection with practical obedience. "Thou shalt keep the commandments of the LORD thy God, to walk in his ways, and to fear him" (Deut. 8:6). "Fear God, and keep his commandments: for this is the whole duty of man" (Eccl. 12:13). God Himself speaks of Job as "one that feareth God, and escheweth evil" (Job 1:8). Inasmuch as a man fears God, he will avoid sin and aim to be holy.

The grace of thankfulness tends to holy practice. Genuine thankfulness leads us to render again according to the benefits we have received. This holds true in earthly relationships—how much more toward God! No man can be truly thankful to God for the dying love of Christ, and for the infinite mercy of God, and yet lead a wicked life. His gratitude, if sincere, will lead him to be holy.

The grace of heavenly-mindedness tends to holy practice. On the other hand, worldly-mindedness tends to selfish, sinful practice. A man may say that he has been weaned from the love of the world, but if his conduct shows him to pursue the world with as much eagerness as before, and if he continues reluctant to part with his portion of this world for pious and charitable uses, he gives no evidence to his claim.

The grace of love to men tends to holy practice. Again, our profession about this is only as good as our practice. "My little children, let us not love in word, neither in tongue; but in deed and in truth. And hereby we know that we are of the truth, and shall assure our hearts before him" (1 John 3:18–19). If you see a father who never shows care for his children, who disregards their suffering, who does not act to relieve and comfort them, you would scarcely believe that he had anything of a father's love in his heart. Love leads to deeds. The same applies to our disposition toward our neighbor. The apostle summarizes all our duties in these words: "If there be any other commandment, it is briefly comprehended in this saying, namely, Thou shalt love thy neighbour as thyself. Love worketh no ill to his neighbour: therefore love is the fulfilling of the law" (Rom. 13:9–10).

The grace of hope in God tends to holy practice. False hope tends to careless, licentious living. But true hope stirs us up to diligence in serving God. "Every man that hath this hope in him purifieth himself, even as he is pure" (1 John 3:3). The thing we hope for is a holy happiness. The Author of that happiness is holy. The Mediator who secures our happiness is holy.

Thus, just as light has a tendency to shine, so grace in the heart has a tendency to holiness in all of life.

Let us now apply this subject to our own hearts.

*1. This doctrine explains why good works are so much insisted on
in the Word of God as evidence of sincerity in grace.*

Our Lord taught us to "know men by their fruits" (Matt. 7:16). "He
that hath my commandments, and keepeth them, he it is that loveth
me.... If a man love me, he will keep my words.... He that loveth
me not keepeth not my sayings" (John 14:21–24). Every epistle further bears this truth. Good works are the only satisfying evidence
that we truly possess grace in our soul. By our practice we are judged
on earth, and by our practice we will be judged at the last day.

*2. Therefore, let us all examine ourselves whether our grace is real
and sincere.*

Let us diligently and prayerfully consider whether we tend to live
holily from day to day. This consideration ought to make false professors tremble. However, it is more likely that those who are truly
godly will tremble, for they are quick to condemn themselves. But
they should understand that the holy life which, according to Scripture, is characteristic of true believers, is not a sinlessly perfect life.
Rather, a Christian's life may be attended with many imperfections,
and yet be a truly Christian life. To aid in this self-examination, ask
the following questions.

*Has the grace you profess rendered your sins to be loathsome, grievous,
and humbling to you?* Has it led you to mourn before God for them?
Does it greatly burden you that your practice is not better than it is?
When you fall into sin, do you with Job abhor yourself and repent
in dust and ashes? Do you with Paul lament your wretchedness and
pray for deliverance?

Do you habitually dread sinning? Do you not only repent of past
sins, but also dread future sins? And if so, do you dread them because they offend God more than anyone else? Do you view sin as a
mortal enemy? Do you keep watch against it, like Joseph who said,
"How then can I do this great wickedness, and sin against God?"
(Gen. 39:9).

Are you conscious of the beauty of practicing holiness? In the words of our text, do you "rejoice in the truth?" Is God's law your delight? Or do you find His commands grievous?

Do you especially delight in duties that are distinctively Christian, and not simply in worldly morality? Unconverted philosophers have waxed eloquent extolling the virtues of morality, justice, generosity, fortitude, etc. But they remained afar off from Christian humility, self-denial, dependence on God, prayerfulness, and forgiveness. Do you delight in these virtues that belong especially to the gospel, which our Savior exemplified supremely?

Do you hunger and thirst after practical holiness? Is this what you live for, long for, and pray for? Do you think, eat, and breathe holiness?

Do you make an all-out effort to live for God in every respect? Is godliness merely incidental in your busy life, or is it the one great business of your life? Is it your greatest concern? As the business of a soldier is to fight, so the business of a Christian is to be like Christ, holy as He is holy. Do you endeavor to be faithful in every known duty? Like the Psalmist, do you crave to "have respect unto all God's commandments" (119:6)?

Do you desire to know all of your duty? Or do you consider ignorance to be bliss? Can you say with Job, "That which I see not teach thou me" (34:32)? Do you desire to *know* God's will so that you might *do* God's will?

Friend, if you can honestly answer these questions in the affirmative, rest assured you possess true grace in the heart that tends to holiness of life. Though you may fall, you shall rise again by God's mercy. He has begun a good work in you, and He will carry it on until the day of Jesus Christ. Though you be faint like Gideon's army, yet pursuing, you will at last overcome.

12

LOVE IS WILLING TO UNDERGO ALL PERSECUTIONS

Charity . . . beareth all things.
— 1 Corinthians 13:7

This phrase evidently speaks of suffering for the cause of Christ. The apostle already dealt with other kinds of injuries from our fellow-man under the words "charity suffereth long" (v. 4) and "is not easily provoked" (v. 5). He seems to have summarized the more active fruits of love with the words of verse 6, "Rejoiceth not in iniquity, but rejoiceth in the truth." He is not now merely repeating himself. Rather, he is setting forth the universal benefit of a spirit of love.

Furthermore, in other passages he connects Christian love with suffering for the name of Christ. For example, in 2 Corinthians 5:14, after telling of some of his sufferings for Christ, he gives the reason: "the love of Christ constraineth us." Elsewhere he declares that tribulation, distress, persecution, and sword cannot separate us from the love of Christ (Rom. 8:35). All this leads us to conclude that the point of our text is that *love, or a truly Christian spirit, will make us willing for Christ's sake to undergo all sufferings to which we may be exposed in the path of duty.*

I. An explanation of this doctrine

Those who have the spirit of love are willing not only to labor but also to suffer for Christ. This is one of the features that distinguishes the genuine believer from the hypocrite. The hypocrite makes a great show of religion in words and actions that costs him nothing. He embraces Christ only inasmuch as he will personally profit. He follows Christ only when he perceives some personal temporal interest. But according to Christ, a true disciple "bears his cross and comes after me" (Luke 14:27).

Those who have the spirit of love are willing to undergo all sufferings which may come upon them as a Christian. They are willing to undergo all *kinds* of sufferings. They willingly face hatred, loss of possessions, torture, and every conceivable suffering, even death. In all these they prove themselves faithful "in much patience, in afflictions, in necessities, in distresses, in stripes, in imprisonments, in tumults, in labours, in watchings, in fastings" (2 Cor. 6:4–5). Also, they are willing to undergo all *degrees* of sufferings. They will walk into the hottest furnace. A true Christian must be willing not only to suffer mockings, but "cruel mockings"; not only loss, but "the loss of all things"; not only death, but the most tormenting methods of death such as being "sawn asunder" (Heb. 11:36–37; Phil. 3:8).

II. Proof of the truth of this doctrine

If we do not have such a spirit, we give evidence of never having given ourselves unreservedly to Christ. Like a bride gives up herself in marriage to her husband to be his and his only, so the soul who closes with Christ offers himself up to Christ as a living sacrifice completely devoted to him. But the one who is not willing to suffer all things for His sake makes an incomplete surrender and reserves to himself some personal ease or interest. He acts as if self were the supreme good, not God.

If we are true Christians, we will so fear God that displeasing Him will be a greater terror to us than suffering any earthly affliction. We see this principle both in the Old Testament as well as the New. "Sanctify the LORD of hosts himself; and let him be your fear, and let him be your dread" (Isa. 8:13). "Be not afraid of them that kill the body, and after that have no more that they can do. But I will forewarn you whom ye shall fear: Fear him, which after he hath killed hath power to cast into hell; yea, I say unto you, Fear him" (Luke 12:4–5).

The faith of a Christian enables him to endure all persecutions. He recognizes that Christ more than makes up for any inconvenience or pain. Hebrews chapter 11 emphasizes that it was by faith that Moses chose "to suffer affliction with the people of God, rather than to enjoy the pleasures of sin for a season; esteeming the reproach of Christ greater riches than the treasures in Egypt: for he had respect unto the recompence of the reward" (v. 25–26). "Likewise, we must have faith to see that our light affliction, which is but for a moment, worketh for us a far more exceeding and eternal weight of glory" (2 Cor. 4:17).

Those who are not willing to follow Christ, regardless of the difficulties, will be overwhelmed with shame in the end. Our Lord taught that there is a cost to being His disciple. "For which of you, intending to build a tower, sitteth not down first, and counteth the cost, whether he have sufficient to finish it? . . . So likewise, whosoever he be of you that forsaketh not all that he hath, he cannot be my disciple" (Luke 14:28, 33). Part of the cost of being His disciple is to suffer in the way of duty. He that does not receive the gospel with all its difficulties does not receive it at all. He that does not receive Christ with His cross as well as His crown, does not truly receive Him at all. If we try to take His rest without His yoke (Matt. 11:29), we accept what He never offered. Those who take only the easy part of Christianity are at best only *almost* Christians.

Without the spirit of our text, we cannot be said to have forsaken all for Christ. He demands that we forsake all for His sake, as duty requires it. But if we refuse to suffer reproach, poverty, pain, or death, we evidence that we have not forsaken honor, wealth, ease, or life for Him.

Without the spirit of our text, we cannot be said to deny ourselves as Scripture requires. Self-denial is plainly taught by our Master. "If any man will come after me, let him deny himself, and take up his cross, and follow me. For whosoever will save his life shall lose it: and whosoever will lose his life for my sake shall find it" (Matt. 16:24–25). To deny yourself is to act as though you had no mercy on yourself. If you disobey Christ in order to avoid suffering, you are denying Christ instead of denying self. All who deny Christ here will be denied by Him hereafter. "If we deny him, he also will deny us" (2 Tim. 2:12).

It is the character of all true Christians that they follow Christ in all things. They "follow the Lamb whithersoever he goeth" (Rev. 14:4), whether in prosperity or adversity. Their attitude is expressed in the words of Ittai to David, "Surely in what place my lord the king shall be, whether in death or life, even there also will thy servant be" (2 Sam. 15:21). To the one who said, "Master, I will follow thee whithersoever thou goest," our Lord responded, "The foxes have holes, and the birds of the air have nests; but the Son of man hath not where to lay his head," indicating that he must follow Christ through great difficulties and sufferings (Matt. 8:19–20).

It is the character of all true Christians that they overcome the world (1 John 5:4). The world seeks to overcome us by both flatteries and frowns. If either of these weapons overcomes us, we simply prove we are not born of God. The true Christian conquers, and more than conquers, in all these things (Rom. 8:37).

Persecution is often called temptation or trial in Scripture, because by it God tries the sincerity of our character. He puts us to the test to prove we are real gold and not a mere counterfeit. "Now for a season, if need be, ye are in heaviness through manifold temptations: that the trial of your faith, being much more precious than of gold that perisheth, though it be tried with fire, might be found unto praise and honour and glory at the appearing of Jesus Christ" (1 Peter 1:6-7). By trials, we prove what we profess. We prove to be His people. "I will refine them as silver is refined, and will try them as gold is tried: they shall call on my name, and I will hear them: I will say, It is my people: and they shall say, The LORD is my God" (Zech. 13:9).

Let us mark the following points by way of application.

1. Let us examine ourselves whether we are willing to undergo all sufferings for Christ.

Do you possess a suffering spirit? Even though you may not have experienced extreme suffering, surely you have lived enough to know whether or not you have a disposition to renounce your own comfort and ease rather than forsake Christ. Every Christian must have a martyr's spirit. Every Christian is tried in some way. Some will suffer in the loss of their good name or in the loss of the good-will of others; some will suffer in their estates or in their business. If you cannot bear these lesser trials, what will become of you if God exposes you to bitter persecution? How can you claim to have the love that "beareth all things?"

2. Let us be prepared to undergo all sufferings for Christ.

Consider the happiness of those who suffer for Christ. Scripture frequently teaches us this: "Blessed are they which are persecuted for righteousness' sake: for theirs is the kingdom of heaven. Blessed are ye, when men shall hate you, and when they shall separate you from their company, and shall reproach you, and cast out your name as evil, for the Son of man's sake. Rejoice ye in that day, and leap for joy: for, behold, your reward is great in heaven. Blessed is the man that endureth temptation: for when he is tried, he shall receive the crown of life, which the Lord hath promised to them that love him. If ye suffer for righteousness' sake, happy are ye" (Matt. 5:10; Luke 6:22–23; James 1:12; 1 Peter 3:14).

Consider the great rewards God has promised to those who willingly suffer for Christ. One verse just quoted speaks of "the crown of life." Others speak of inheriting everlasting life, being counted worthy of the kingdom of God, reigning with Him, and being glorified together with Him. The greatest and most glorious things are promised to those who overcome, according to Revelation chapters 2 and 3, including sitting with Christ on His throne! Who would not gladly "bear all things in order to gain such glorious rewards?"

Consider the many examples in the Scripture of people who suffered for Christ. The Psalmist makes frequent references to his enemies, such as "Princes have persecuted me without a cause: but my heart standeth in awe of thy word" (119:161). Jeremiah was threatened with death and put in a stinking dungeon. Daniel continued to pray even though he would be cast into a den of lions. Time would fail me to tell of all who are in this great cloud of witnesses. Do you think any of them have any regrets now? Most of all, consider the supreme example of our Lord Himself who suffered beyond compare, was faithful to the end, and is now exalted to highest station. Therefore, "let us lay aside every weight, and the sin which doth so easily beset us, and let us run with patience the race that is set before us, Looking unto Jesus the author and finisher of our faith; who for the joy that was set before him endured the cross, despising the shame, and is set down at the right hand of the throne of God" (Heb. 12:1–2). "Be thou faithful unto death, and I will give thee a crown of life" (Rev. 2:10).

13

ALL THE GRACES OF LOVE CONNECTED

Charity . . . believeth all things, hopeth all things.
— 1 Corinthians 13:7

As with the previous phrase, we must be sure what subject the apostle is addressing. Many think him to be saying that love *believes the best and hopes for the best with respect to our neighbor.* However, he has already treated that subject under the words of verse 5, "thinketh no evil." He seems to have finished dealing with the fruits of love toward our neighbor with the summarizing words of verse 6, "Rejoiceth not in iniquity, but rejoiceth in the truth." He mentions in our text the same triad of graces mentioned again in verse 13—faith, hope, and love. The whole drift of the chapter is to show the relation of love to other graces. For these reasons, I take these two phrases of our text to say, that *love promotes the exercise of all graces, especially the graces of faith and hope.* In other words, *all the graces of Christianity are connected together and mutually dependent.* Like links of a chain they all hang together. If one is broken, they all fall to the ground.

I. How all Christian graces are connected

All Christian graces always go together. Where one is, all are. Where one is not, none are. For example, 1 John tells us that love to the brethren is a sign of love to God, and on the other hand, love to God is a sign of love to the brethren. "If a man say, I love God, and hateth his brother, he is a liar. . . . By this we know that we love the children of God, when we love God, and keep his commandments" (4:20; 5:2).

All Christian graces depend on one another. For example, faith promotes love, in that we cannot love one whose existence we doubt. Yet love is the most effectual ingredient in a living faith; for we are more likely to believe someone we love than someone we do not love. Likewise, faith begets hope, and hope strengthens faith. Furthermore, love tends to hope, and hope promotes love. Faith promotes humility, and humility serves faith. Love and humility mutually promote each other. Love tends to repentance. Repentance, faith and love all tend to thankfulness. On and on we could go with every Christian grace.

Every Christian grace in some way implies the others. Faith implies humility, for we cannot conceive of a proud faith. Faith implies love: "faith . . worketh by love" (Gal. 5:6). Faith and repentance imply each other, seeing they describe the same act of the soul in turning from sin to Christ. The fear of God implies love, for it is not a slavish fear of which we speak, but a childlike fear. How many graces assume the presence of patience! Again, we could multiply the examples almost endlessly.

II. Why Christian graces are thus connected

They all stem from the same source. "There are diversities of operations, but it is the same God which worketh all in all" (1 Cor. 12:6). Just as the whole spectrum of colors comes from only one ray of light, so all graces are from the same Holy Spirit of God. The differences between them, whereby they have different names, are more relative than absolute, more in reference to their various objects and modes of exercise than from a real difference in their abstract nature.

They are all communicated in the same work of the Holy Spirit, namely, conversion. There is not one conversion of the soul to faith, another conversion to loving God, another conversion to loving man, another conversion to humility, and yet another to repentance. All the graces are given to us in regeneration. In this, the spiritual birth is like our physical birth: we received all our faculties like seeing, hearing and tasting, at one time in one birth.

They all have the same root and foundation, namely, the knowledge of God's excellence. One genuine sight of God begets all graces—faith, repentance, love, hope, etc. If we truly know God's nature, we will love Him, trust Him, submit to Him, and manifest every other grace. "They that know thy name will put their trust in thee" (Ps. 9:10).

They all have the same rule, namely, the law of God. He who has a true respect to one of God's commands must have a respect to all of them. They are all established by the same authority and reflect the same holy nature of God. In like manner, to offend in one point of the law is to break every point, regardless of how many points you keep (James 2:10).

They all have the same end, namely, God Himself. Not only do they spring from Him, stand on Him, and find direction from Him, but they also point to Him. His glory and our happiness in Him is the great end of all graces. This shows that they are all closely related.

They are all related to one and the same grace as the sum of them all, namely, love. We considered this in chapter one. No matter how many different names we give them, and no matter how different the modes of their exercise, all Christian graces are resolved into one: love. Love is the fulfilling of them all. This is another reason why all the graces are connected.

Now let us endeavor to make practical application of this truth.

1. The connection of all graces should aid our understanding of old things being done away and all things becoming new in conversion.

This is what the apostle speaks of in 2 Corinthians 5:17, "If any man be in Christ, he is a new creature: old things are passed away; behold, all things are become new." All graces of Christianity are imparted in some measure at conversion. A true believer, the moment he is converted, possesses all gracious dispositions. They may be feeble, but still they are present, like a baby whose parts and powers are all present, though in a weak form. There are as many graces in every believer as there were in Jesus Christ Himself, and thus John the apostle writes, "And of his fulness have all we received, and grace for grace" (John 1:16). We "have put on the new man, which is renewed in knowledge after the image of him that created him" (Col. 3:10). Before conversion, we possessed no graces, but after conversion we possess every grace, albeit in an imperfect form. Perhaps this is why we are said to be new men in Christ Jesus, not just new eyes or new ears.

It follows, therefore, that every corruption in a believer is mortified, albeit in an imperfect measure. For every sin there is a grace that answers to it. Faith tends to mortify unbelief. Love mortifies enmity. Humility mortifies pride. Meekness mortifies revenge, etc. All old things pass away, though imperfectly on this earth; and all things become new, though also imperfectly. Thus, we see what a great work and what a great change conversion is.

2. We may test our hope of salvation by testing one grace with another.

If you profess to have come to Christ in faith, you should ask whether your faith was accompanied by repentance and humility. Or did you come to Christ with a proud, pharisaical spirit, presenting your own goodness? Did love accompany your faith?

On the other hand, you profess to love Christ. But did faith accompany your love? Did you embrace the conviction that Christ is the very Son of God, the only, the glorious, and the all-sufficient Savior? If not, your love for Christ is no better than the love for a fictitious character in a novel.

You profess to have the grace of hope. Does faith accompany it? Is your hope grounded on the conviction of the truth concerning Christ, His worthiness, and His alone? Does your hope include humility, or are you proud of yourself in the hope you entertain? Does the grace of obedience accompany your hope? False hope flatters the heart and hardens it in disobedience.

You profess love for God. But this too must be tested by other graces. Has your love of the world diminished simply because of some outward affliction that hinders you from enjoying the world? Perhaps your professed love for God stems from some distress of conscience, and you manage to tear yourself away from the world while your heart still cleaves to it as much as ever. Or are you truly weaned from the love of the world because an Object higher and better has captured your heart and you cannot love the world anymore?

You may further test your love to God by your love to the people of God. How many people profess to love God, but are destitute of godly dispositions toward men? And how many appear to be kind, generous and good toward men, but lack a right disposition toward God? False grace is like a defective work of art in which some essential part is lacking. Using another figure, God complained of Ephraim that he was "a cake not turned" (Hos. 7:8), that is, burnt on one side, but raw on the other, and therefore good for nothing. We must carefully avoid such an uneven character and be consistent, proportioned Christians, growing in every grace "unto the measure of the stature of the fullness of Christ" (Eph. 4:13).

14

LOVE NOT TO BE
OVERTHROWN BY OPPOSITION

Charity . . . endureth all things.
— *1 Corinthians 13:7*

W e should not assume that with this phrase the apostle is simply restating what he already said in verse 4, "charity suffereth long," or at the beginning of the present verse, "charity beareth all things." All three of these statements address different matters. As we have seen, the first reference speaks of patiently bearing general injuries. The second reference speaks of suffering persecution as a Christian. In the present text, the principle is that *love cannot be overthrown by anything that opposes it.* In other words, true Christian grace will endure notwithstanding all the opposition that may be brought against it.

I. There is much opposition against grace in the heart of a Christian.

Enemies against the principle of grace in a child of God are legion. We are compassed about on every side. We are pilgrims passing through enemy country, exposed to attack at every moment. The Devil and his demons are our bitter enemies. The world tempts us in a variety of ways. We also carry within us a vast number of enemies, in our thoughts and inclinations. So many and so strong are all these enemies that the Christian life is often called a warfare. All these enemies are irreconcilable to us, sworn in their bitter animosity to ruin and overthrow the work of grace within us. Sometimes one enemy, and sometimes another, and sometimes all of them together carry out an assault against us. Like a flood, they come seeking to overwhelm us and swallow us up. God's work of grace, summarized in *love*, is exposed like a spark of fire in the midst of a storm.

But now let us consider the truth of our text.

II. All the opposition against grace in the heart cannot overthrow it.

That is not to say that the enemies of our soul do not gain great advantages against us. They may bring the work of grace in us to the very brink of utter ruin. The lion may come against the lamb with a great roar and with an open mouth. He may take the lamb in his very paw. Yea, he may actually swallow him down, as the whale swallowed Jonah, yet like Jonah, it shall be brought up again, and live. Many Scriptures illustrate this truth. Israel was surrounded at the Red Sea, and all appeared hopeless, yet God delivered them. David was separated from death by only one step, yet God preserved him. The boat in which our Lord lay asleep was about to sink, but God made it to stay afloat. Even so, the gates of hell can never prevail against Christ's church, nor can they prevail against grace in our heart. Our seed remains in us (1 John 3:9), and nothing can root it out. In the end, grace subdues all its enemies under its feet. The present humiliations only prepare it for future exaltation.

Now let us consider two reasons why all opposition cannot overthrow grace in the heart.

First, true grace, unlike false grace, contains in its very nature that which tends to perseverance. False grace is only superficial and outward, but true grace reaches the bottom of the heart and involves a change of nature that endures. False grace does not mortify sin, but leaves it alive and well. True grace strikes a deadly blow to sin. Counterfeit grace may affect the emotions, but genuine grace involves thorough conviction in the very foundation of the soul.

Second, God upholds true grace once He has implanted it in the soul. He simply will not allow opposition to overthrow it. We are not kept from falling by the inherent nature of grace by itself, but "by the power of God" Himself (1 Peter 1:5). After all, Adam and Eve possessed holiness with no inward corruption, yet it was overthrown. Considering a believer's indwelling corruption, we see how greatly we need God to uphold grace in us.

God does indeed uphold grace in us because He has promised to do so. "Though he fall, he shall not be utterly cast down: for the LORD upholdeth him with his hand. I will make an everlasting covenant with them, that I will not turn away from them, to do them good; but I will put my fear in their hearts, that they shall not depart from me. And this is the Father's will which hath sent me, that of all which he hath given me I should lose nothing, but should raise it up again at the last day. I give unto them eternal life; and they shall never perish. He which hath begun a good work in you will perform it until the day of Jesus Christ. He is able to keep us from falling, and to present us faultless before the presence of his glory with exceeding joy." His purpose extends from foreknowing and predestinating us, to calling and justifying us, and finally to glorifying us forever (Ps. 37:24; Jer. 32:40; John 6:39; 10:28; Phil. 1:6; Jude 24; Rom. 8:29–30).

Why will God uphold the work of grace in us, and not allow any opposition to defeat it? Here are seven answers to this question.

First, Christ's redemption has secured our persevering. Otherwise, it would not be a complete redemption. If our persevering depended on ourselves alone, how could we expect to do any better than unfallen Adam?

Second, the covenant of grace was introduced to supply what was lacking in the first covenant. The main thing lacking in the covenant with Adam was a sure ground of perseverance in godliness. Man's will was the only ground for it, and thus it was liable to change. But God ordained another covenant, better than the first because it is more enduring. It cannot fail and is repeatedly called *an everlasting covenant*. The head and surety of the first covenant was liable to fail, but God provided as the head and surety of the new covenant One who cannot fail. With Christ as our representative, this covenant is *ordered in all things and sure.*

Third, since God's covenant in Christ is one of grace, it is not fitting that the reward of life be suspended on man's strength to persevere. Rather, free and sovereign grace undertakes for us. We are not left to the power of our own will, but to the power of the God of all grace.

Fourth, Christ as our Surety has already persevered, overcome, and conquered. Since He has already fulfilled the terms of the covenant, the final perseverance of His people is certain.

Fifth, the doctrine of justification assures that all of a man's sins are put away once and forever. They cannot be brought up against him in heaven's court. Justification does not depend on our perseverance; our perseverance flows from our justification.

Sixth, the Scriptures teach that the believer's life is in Christ and derives from vital union with Him. He "hath quickened us together with Christ, (by grace ye are saved;) and hath raised us up together, and made us sit together in heavenly places in Christ Jesus" (Eph. 2:5–6). "I am crucified with Christ: nevertheless I live; yet not I, but Christ liveth in me" (Gal. 2:20). Since Christ "ever liveth" and is "alive forevermore," and since "death hath no more dominion over him" (Heb. 7:25; Rev. 1:18; Rom. 6:9), our spiritual life cannot but continue!

Seventh, Christ introduced the principle of grace in our hearts in spite of great opposition. Enemies to grace are nothing new. But if His almighty power has triumphantly brought in grace, the same power will sustain it and not allow it to fail.

As we seek to apply this precious doctrine, let us mark the following points.

1. We learn one reason why the devil so fiercely opposes the conversion of sinners.

He knows that once they are converted, once grace dwells in their souls, they are beyond the reach of his destroying power, and he cannot overthrow them. Therefore, he is always active, violently opposing those who are awakened, or under conviction, or seeking Christ. He does all he possibly can to quench their conviction of sin and make them happy in sin. He sometimes flatters them; then he turns and discourages them. He leads them to quarrel with God. Some he tempts with an abuse of the truth concerning God's decrees, resorting to fatalism. Some he tempts with fears of the unpardonable sin. Some he deceives with false assurance of salvation. His methods are almost innumerable, and he vigorously uses them, for he knows he cannot overthrow a true convert to Christ.

2. We learn that those whose grace fails never truly possessed grace.

Many people seem much affected at first by the truth, but when the novelty is over, they return to their old ways. They only prove that they were strangers to grace all along. They fail to prove 2 Corinthians 5:17, "If any man be in Christ, he is a new creation." They are like the promise of many springtime blossoms on the trees–they fall off and never bear fruit. The test and proof of grace is continuance or *enduring all things*. The grace that does not hold out and persevere is not real grace.

3. The truth of our text gives cause for great joy and comfort for those who have good evidence of grace in their heart.

Grace is a precious jewel, and for those who possess it, it is a jewel that can never be taken away. The One who gave it to us will keep it for us by His mighty power by which "he is able even to subdue all things unto himself" (Phil. 3:21). His everlasting arms are underneath us. He is our refuge and strength. Therefore, no matter how subtle and violent the attacks against us may be, we can laugh our foes to scorn, standing on the rock of our salvation. Here is cause for rejoicing!

4. The truth of our text affords encouragement to the saints in their spiritual warfare.

If a solider goes into battle expecting to be defeated, his enemy has all but won already. But the Captain of our salvation has assured us victory. His promise is sure and cannot fail. Onward to the fight, child of God! Resting on His promise, be faithful in your part, and soon you will sing the song of victory. Soon He will place on your head, with His nail-scarred hands, the crown of victory.

15

THE HOLY SPIRIT FOREVER COMMUNICATED TO BELIEVERS IN THE GRACE OF LOVE

Charity never faileth: but whether there be prophecies,
they shall fail; whether there be tongues, they shall cease;
whether there be knowledge, it shall vanish away.
— 1 Corinthians 13:8

Thus far we have seen the superiority of love over all other Christian graces. All other gifts are nothing without it. It is the source of all good dispositions and behavior. It is the most durable of all gifts.

In our text, the apostle says two things.

First, love will *never fail*; it lasts forever. The *enduring of all things* (v. 7) implies and leads to this *never failing*.

Second, all other gifts will indeed fail. He mentions three gifts: (1) *prophecy*, or words directly inspired by the Holy Spirit; (2) *tongues*, or the power to speak in languages that one had never learned, as on the day of Pentecost; (3) *knowledge*, or the miraculous gift of understanding, called the *word of knowledge* in chapter 12, verse 8. This term cannot refer to all knowledge, for our knowledge of God shall continue to increase in heaven. This special gift of knowledge stands in contrast to the knowledge that is acquired from reason and study, and the experiential knowledge of the saving influence of the Holy Spirit in the soul.

These three gifts were previously mentioned in verses 1 and 2 as being nothing without the grace of love. They were examples of extraordinary gifts bestowed for the infancy of Christianity while it was being introduced and established in the earth. When this purpose was accomplished, all these extraordinary gifts were to *fail* and *cease*. But the ordinary and better grace of love was never to cease.

Plainly then, the doctrine of our text is that *the great fruit of the Holy Spirit, in which He will everlastingly be communicated to God's people, is charity or godly love.*

I. The Holy Spirit is given to God's people everlastingly to indwell and influence them.

The Holy Spirit is the chief and sum of all the good things that Christ has purchased for us in this life and in the life to come. He is the purchase and promise of Christ for His church, so that she may continue, and so that the gates of hell may not prevail against her. "And I will pray the Father, and he shall give you another Comforter, that he may abide with you for ever; even the Spirit of truth; whom the world cannot receive, because it seeth him not, neither knoweth him: but ye know him; for he dwelleth with you, and shall be in you" (John 14:16-17). Adam, in his original state, had the Holy Spirit, yet lost it by his disobedience. But in the new covenant, God imparts the Holy Spirit in a more permanent way, so as never to depart.

II. There are other gifts of the Spirit besides those summarized in love, wherein the Holy Spirit is communicated to God's people.

These fall into two categories.

First, by the extraordinary gifts, such as miracles and inspiration, the Holy Spirit has been communicated to God's people. We read of these gifts in operation at certain seasons in the Old Testament as well as in greater frequency in the days of the early church.

Second, by gifts of common grace the Holy Spirit is communicated to both lost and saved people. There are common convictions of sin, common illuminations, and common religious affections, which, though they have nothing in them of true Christian love or saving grace, yet they are the fruits of the Spirit in that they are the effect of His influences on the hearts of men.

III. All these other gifts of the Spirit last but for a season, and either have ceased or shall cease.

The extraordinary gifts of the Spirit, such as prophecy, tongues, and knowledge, most certainly ceased with the apostles themselves. They were no longer needed, seeing that the writing of the New Testament books was finished. The apostle John indicates this plainly in the closing words of Revelation, written shortly before his death. The main purpose of extraordinary gifts was to reveal God's truth before it came to be written down. Before Moses, God frequently spoke directly to Adam, Enoch, Noah, Abraham, Isaac, Jacob, and others. Then came long periods of time in which there was little or no direct revelation. After about four hundred years of silence, the Spirit again broke upon the scene with extraordinary gifts to Anna and Simeon, Elizabeth and Zacharias, Mary and Joseph, and John the Baptist. Beginning on the day of Pentecost, we see a remarkable effusion of these gifts in the book of Acts. But once God had given, through the apostles and their close associates, the written revelation of His mind and will, fully recorded as a long-standing rule for His disciples for all ages, the extraordinary gifts ceased. God caused them to cease because there was no further occasion for them. Nor will they exist in heaven, for the same reason.

As for the common operations of the Spirit, though they continue to this day, they will cease to exist after the day of judgment. Their purpose and occasion is limited to this world.

IV. The gift of godly love is the great fruit of the Holy

Spirit that never fails, in which He has and always shall influence His people.

Since the Spirit is given by Christ to His people forever, then regardless of what fruits of the Spirit may be temporary, either for the apostolic age or for all time, there must be some influence of the Spirit that is unfailing and everlasting. Charity, or divine love, is that fruit in which the everlasting influences of the Holy Spirit appear.

We may consider the outworking of this principle in two ways: individually and collectively.

First, every true child of God experiences an ongoing and unending love. As Romans 8:38-39 teaches, nothing "shall be able to separate us from the love of God, which is in Christ Jesus our Lord." This love outlasts our earthly life. When the apostles died, they left their miraculous gifts along with their bodies, but the love that was in their hearts they carried with them to heaven. When wicked men die, they leave behind all the influences of common grace. But when a Christian dies, though he leaves behind many fruits of the Spirit that he had in common with wicked men, yet he takes love with him to eternity, where it is perfected, and where it will live and reign with perfect and glorious dominion in his soul for ever and ever.

Second, this principle of unfailing love applies to all believers collectively. Even though, as we have seen, miraculous gifts came and went during both Testaments, this grace of godly love has been kept up constantly by God among His people. And when this world is done, when all God's elect are settled in their final state, God-like love shall not fail but shall be brought to glorious perfection. Every soul in that company will be, as it were, in a blaze of holy love, and will remain and grow in that love throughout the unending ages of eternity!

Someone may ask, "Why should other fruits of the Spirit fail, while this fruit remains forever?" The answer is because love is the great end of all the other fruits and gifts of the Spirit. The miraculous gifts were but means to this end—to promote holiness and to build up the kingdom of God in the heart, all of which is summarized in *love*. Extraordinary gifts revealed and confirmed the will of God. They were means of grace, but love is the grace itself. The means cease, but the end continues. Likewise, the common gifts of the Spirit, such as illumination and conviction, are only valuable insofar as they tend to promote grace and holiness which consists in love. When love is perfected, they will cease to be necessary.

Now let us mark some lessons we should learn from this text.

1. There is no reason to assume that the extraordinary gifts of the Spirit will be restored in the last days.

Not a few writers past and present have held to this erroneous position which the text and the whole context plainly refute. The latter-day glory of Christ's kingdom on the earth will be more glorious than ever before. It only stands to reason that the "more excellent way" of chapter 12, verse 31, will then prevail, and not a returning to the less excellent way of miraculous gifts. In verses 9 and 10 of our text, the apostle makes it plain that the *partial* gives way to the complete or *perfect*. Prophecy and miracles argue an infantile condition of the church, rather than its maturity. Why then should that which is inferior return in the days of greatest superiority? Why should an adult church return to "childish things"? (v. 11). Surely the history of revivals proves that God's Spirit may work mightily without any return of miraculous gifts. The Spirit of God with the Word of God is sufficient to work effectually to the saving of multitudes of souls. Inasmuch as we need no new Scriptures, we need no return of the miracles that produced and confirmed the Scriptures.

2. We should be extremely cautious in giving heed to anything that appears to be a new revelation or an extraordinary gift of the Spirit.

Some people follow their impressions or dreams as if they were immediate miraculous revelations from God. But according to our text, all such gifts have ceased. Therefore, such supposed revelations are only great deceptions.

3. We should highly prize the fruits of the Spirit, summarized in love, which are evidences of true grace in the soul.

Because of the superiority of ordinary graces, let us earnestly desire and seek this blessed fruit of the Spirit. Let us desire that the love of God may be shed abroad in our hearts more and more. Let us deliberately love our Lord Jesus Christ in sincerity, and love one another as Christ hath loved us. Possessing this grace, we assure our hearts of possessing eternal life, because this grace never fails even unto eternity. Love in our hearts on earth prepares us for heaven, the world of love, where the Spirit of love reigns and blesses forever.

16

HEAVEN A WORLD OF LOVE

Charity never faileth: but whether there be prophecies,
they shall fail; whether there be tongues, they shall cease;
whether there be knowledge, it shall vanish away.
For we know in part, and we prophesy in part.
But when that which is perfect is come,
then that which is in part shall be done away.
— 1 Corinthians 13:8–10

As we have seen, these verses teach that the Holy Spirit will be communicated everlastingly to the people of God through charity or divine love. We further notice that even when all other fruits have ended, love will remain. This will occur when the *partial* state has given way to the *perfect* state.

There is a twofold partial state of God's people and a twofold complete state. In one instance, the primitive order of the New Testament economy was incomplete compared with the mature order that came with the completion of the written revelation. This is like adulthood as contrasted with childhood. In another instance, the present order is yet imperfect in comparison with the order that will exist in the state of glorification. That state will be the maturity of full perfection that will make our present maturity seem childish.

Likewise, there is a twofold failing of the gifts mentioned here. First, the miraculous gifts ceased with the completion of the New Testament canon, for they were no longer needed. Second, the common gifts of the Spirit will fail at the end of the world, for they are designed for this world. But love will continue in the eternal state.

It is the second of these senses that seems to be especially on the mind of the apostle. Therefore, the doctrine we draw from the text is that *heaven is a world of charity or love*. These verses speak of a time when the Holy Spirit will be more abundantly and perfectly given. The way in which He will be given will be through the grace of love in the hearts of all the inhabitants of heaven. Love will be the only gift then needed, seeing it is the most perfect and glorious of all; and once it is brought to perfection, all other gifts will be unnecessary.

I. The cause and source of love in heaven

God is the source of all holy love. He dwells in a special sense in heaven, which is His palace where He gloriously manifests Himself; and, therefore, it follows that He is the fountain of love in heaven. "God is love" (1 John 4:16). As He is infinite, all-sufficient, and immutable, His love is infinite, inexhaustible, and eternal. In heaven dwells the triune God from whom every drop of love proceeds. God the Father dwells there, the Father of mercies who so loved the world that He gave His only begotten Son. God the Son dwells there, who loved us and gave Himself for us. There, in both His divine and human natures, He sits on the same throne with the Father. God the Holy Spirit dwells there, who personally communicates this love to us. All this renders heaven a world of love. This glorious fountain of love flows forth in streams that swell into rivers that swell into an ocean of love, in which the souls of the ransomed may bathe with the sweetest enjoyment, engulfed as it were in floods of holy love.

II. The objects of love in heaven

First, there are none but lovely objects in heaven. "There shall in no wise enter into it any thing that defileth, neither whatsoever worketh abomination, or maketh a lie" (Rev. 21:27). Only holy angels and men are there. No false professors, no pretenders are there, only saints whose gold has been purified of all its dross.

Second, the objects in heaven are perfectly lovely. The very best man on earth, though generally lovely, still has his spots and defects. But in heaven every soul is perfectly pure and lovely. No moral or natural defects enter there. There is no veiling of the Son of God as in His incarnation, but the fullness of His glory will show. Wherever the inhabitants of the blessed world will turn their eyes, they see nothing but dignity, beauty, and glory.

Third, in heaven shall be all the objects upon which the saints have set their hearts above all else, while in this world. Things that delighted their souls, captivated their affections, in which they rejoiced to meditate, for which sake they were willing to undergo great suffering and forsake father, mother, wife, children, and life itself, are all there. Loved ones in the Lord who were snatched by death are there. We will enjoy the company of patriarchs and apostles and all those whom we have known only by faith. Above all, we will enjoy and dwell with God, who is altogether lovely, and we will be filled with all His fullness forever.

III. The subjects of love in heaven

Here, we speak of those who are the lovers. Love dwells and reigns in every heart in heaven. It begins with God the Father, who is the original source of all love. From Him it proceeds to the Son, who is both the object and subject of infinite love. He is the Beloved of the Father, who also perfectly loves the Father. This love is a mutual holy energy between the Father and Son—a pure and holy act whereby the deity becomes, as it were, one infinite and unchangeable emotion of love.

This love also flows out to all the created beings in heaven. All those who are in Christ were beloved before the foundation of the world, but they also become subjects of love, reflecting the love of God as planets reflect the light of the sun. The only souls in heaven are souls that supremely love God with a perfect heart.

All the persons in the glorious society of heaven are sincerely united in love. The heart of God and of men and of angels goes out to all the others there. Each person sees the loveliness of the others with a full delight. The love is mutual, full, and eternal.

IV. The principle of love itself in heaven

First, the nature of this love is altogether holy and divine. Much of what we call love now is carnal and proceeds from corrupt principles and motives or is directed to corrupt ends. But the love of heaven is spiritual, directed by holy motives to holy ends. The love of heaven is a love for God's sake and for the sake of the relation that persons have to Him.

Second, the degree of this love is perfect. God's love is perfect, and the love of others in heaven is perfect as far as their capacity as creatures is concerned. There is no pride or selfishness to hinder love in heaven—no enmity, no envy, no contempt. The love of benevolence finds delight in beholding the happiness of another, and the love of complacence finds delight in beholding the beauty and perfection of another. It will not be a grief to any saint to see those that are higher than himself in holiness and that are most loved by others, for he will rejoice with them with a benevolent love. Every man shall be perfectly satisfied with God and with his own personal measure of glory. The most glorious shall be the most humble, so that pride can find no place to occupy. The least glorious will not be envious, due to the fact that those above them are more humble. With perfect love in every soul, there simply cannot be any spiritual class warfare in heaven.

V. Ways in which love is exercised in heaven

1. It is mutual. Love always seeks a return, and in heaven it will be fully satisfied without any slighting. God's love to us will satisfy us more than it presently does. His love to us is not a return, properly speaking, since He loved us first. Nevertheless, the sight of His love will fill us with joy, admiration, and love to Him. Thus, He says, "I love them that love me" (Prov. 8:17). Also, the love between saints will always be reciprocal.

2. It cannot be interrupted by jealousy. The love will be so sincere that none need fear flattery or hypocrisy. It will be as though a window were open in every breast, so that the whole heart can be seen. Everyone will be what he appears to be. There will be no suspicion or fear of a weakening of love. The saints will know that the love of God will continue without change.

3. It cannot be hindered by anything within the saints themselves. On this earth, we find much to hinder our love, including our very body, which clogs our expressions of love by its limitations and demands on us. But in heaven there is no dullness or heaviness. We will be at perfect liberty to express our love.

4. It will be expressed with perfect decency and wisdom. Sometimes on this earth, love is obscured by a person's indiscreet expressions of it. But in heaven, wisdom, and discretion will be perfected along with love.

5. It cannot be hindered by anything external to the inhabitants. There will be no distance, no misunderstandings, no disunion. But all will be united in the same interests of serving and glorifying the same God.

6. It will unite every person together in a near and dear relationship. Every inhabitant will be a child of God, and thus all will be related to each other as brethren. There will be only one family in heaven: the household of God.

7. It will operate in mutual property and ownership of each other. Love longs for ownership. The language of love is, "My beloved is mine, and I am his" (Song 2:16). We will belong to God as His treasure, and He will belong to us as our inheritance and portion, according to His covenant mercy. Moreover, if saints belong to each other now, how much more in the glorified state! "They . . . gave their own selves . . . unto us by the will of God" (2 Cor. 8:5).

8. It will be enjoyed in perfect and uninterrupted prosperity. On earth, adversity, poverty, and affliction often hinder love, as we grieve for ourselves or for others. But in heaven, we shall all reign as kings and priests unto God forever, inheriting all things. We will enjoy not only our own prosperity, but also that of others, as we partake of each other's joy. We will so share in the joy of others that it will be as though it were our own.

9. It will be promoted by the working together of all things. Everything about heaven lends itself to be a source of enjoyment. Everything is suited to work together to our advantage. There is no division. The petty distinctions of this world do not draw lines in the society of heaven, but all meet in the equality of holiness and of holy love. Heaven is a garden of pleasures, where all things point to God, who is the light of the whole place. "And the city had no need of the sun, neither of the moon, to shine in it: for the glory of God did lighten it, and the Lamb is the light thereof" (Rev. 21:23).

10. It will be enjoyed with the knowledge that it will continue forever. No change occurs there, unless it be for the better. Neither the love nor the objects of it will grow old or wear away. All will flourish in immortal youth and freshness. The pleasure of heaven will be like a living spring perpetually supplying our souls, like a river that ever flows and increases, like a perpetual springtime that never fades into winter. The trees of heaven yield their fruit every month (Rev. 22:2). No night will settle on the brightness of everlasting day.

VI. The happy effects of love in heaven

We mention only two among many.

First, consider the perfect behavior of all the inhabitants of heaven toward God and toward each other. All sin and its effects will be excluded. Therefore, all our behavior will be perfect. None will come short or turn aside from perfect obedience to God. Every part of our behavior will be holy in matter, form, spirit, and end. In some way or another, we will praise and serve God continually, perhaps by serving one another in that great united society.

Second, consider the perfect tranquility and joy in heaven. Love tends to quiet and calm the soul. It removes disturbances and brings a happy composition. In a place of perfect love, there will be no storms, not even a threatening cloud! In this world, we see many principles contrary to love: selfishness, envy, revenge, and the like. But in heaven, there is no enemy and no enmity, nothing to disturb or offend or cause conflict and contention; only perfect harmony and purity. There are no differing judgments or opinions, no busybodies to spoil the perfect peace.

What a joy to enter this haven of rest, this sweet calm, after having passed through the storms and tempests of this violent and furious world! What a Canaan to enter after the waste howling wilderness full of snares and serpents, where no rest could be found! Here we enjoy streams of sweetness, but there, an ocean. We will stand before God with hearts open to be filled with the fullness of His love. Every soul will be like a note in a symphony that sweetly harmonizes with all the other notes in the most rapturous strains of praise to God and the Lamb forever. We will pour our love back into the great Fountain of love by which we are supplied. Our joy will be ever increasing yet ever full. Such a scene eye hath not seen, nor ear heard, neither hath entered into the heart of man. Yet nothing less than this is what the people loved by God shall enjoy for ever and ever!

In conclusion, let us apply this grand subject.

1. If heaven is such a world as we have described, then we see why contention and strife darken our evidence of being fit for that place.

A spirit of contention darkens our assurance of salvation. It removes the tranquility of heaven from our hearts. Our communion with God is interrupted. Discord between husband and wife causes their prayers to be hindered (1 Peter 3:7). When we are contentious, we are least prepared for heaven, and have least evidence of a title to it.

2. The people destined for heaven are truly happy.

There are some people living on earth even now, to whom the happiness of heaven is as much a possession as is any earthly estate to a mortal man. Those who have this title to heaven are truly the happiest people on earth. Who are these people? Let us consider their character in three areas.

First, they are those that have had the principle of heavenly love implanted in their hearts by regeneration. They are not simply born with a great degree of natural love, but they are born again and possess a supernatural love. It is a glorious work, as though the Holy Spirit brought down to their souls some of the love of heaven.

Second, they are those who have freely chosen the happiness of heaven above all other conceivable happiness. They are convinced not just by rational arguments but by a personal tasting of it. Love to God and love to godly persons, communion with God and with godly persons, is what they relish above all else. They more eagerly pursue this than anything else. They have not chosen it simply because it is an alternative to this present life of sorrow and trouble. Rather, they would choose it even if this life were full of unending earthly happiness.

Third, they are those who, from a principle of divine love, struggle after holiness. Holy love makes them long for holiness. Nevertheless, they struggle because sin tends to keep them from this holiness, this fruitfulness, this deepening experience of communion with God. The Christian never feels that his heart or his hands are holy enough. His struggle is not just due to fear, but is due to love's desire for perfection. Holy love longs for liberation from sin.

3. The impenitent ought to be awakened and alarmed.

First, they ought to be so affected because they have no portion or right in this world of love. They will never know this blessed, perfect, glorious state. As Nehemiah said to Sanballat's company, "Ye have no portion, nor right, nor memorial, in Jerusalem" (Neh. 2:20). If an unrepentant soul were allowed into heaven, it would be nauseating to the happy souls there. Heaven would no longer be heaven. Instead of a world of love, it would become a world of hatred, pride, envy, malice, and revenge, like this present world.

Second, they ought to be so affected because they are in danger of hell, a world of hatred. There are three worlds: one of love, one of hatred, and the present one, which is a mixture, which proves that it cannot continue forever. In hell, not one object is lovely or amiable; nothing is pure, holy, or pleasant. Everything is detestable, loathsome, horrid, abominable, odious, and hateful. It is a den of poisonous hissing serpents, Satan and all his hateful brood.

God hates everyone in hell with a perfect hatred. He exercises no love and extends no mercy to any object there, but He pours out to them horrors without mixture. God made hell as a testimony forever of His hatred of sin and sinners. Hell is a world overflowed with wrath, a deluge of liquid fire, so as to be called a lake of fire.

All the inhabitants of hell hate God. They will never feel any love for Him. Further, they hate each other. The only point of agreement between the inmates is their blasphemy and rage against God. The demons of hell will continue to torment men in hell just as they did in this life. And men will continue to act like devils toward their fellow-man.

In hell, pride, malice, envy, revenge, and everything opposed to love and peace will be unrestrained. God will exercise no restraining grace. Whereas sinners here were companions together in their sin, there they will have no appearance of fellowship. As they promoted each other's sins here, there they will promote each other's punishment.

If you are in sin, outside of Christ, never born again, a stranger to true love and holiness, then consider this: this is the world to which you will be condemned by the righteous judgment of God. Unless you repent, you will see these dreadful realities forever. How can you rest in your present state? How can you so neglect your soul with eternity always in view? Flee at once to the stronghold of redemption in Jesus Christ before the door of hope is closed, and your doom sealed, and your agonies begun.

4. Let us all earnestly seek after heaven.

This glorious world of love is offered to us, and it is not impossible but that it may be obtained by us. God stands ready to give us an inheritance there, if we truly desire and choose and seek it. God gives us our choice. We will have our inheritance wherever we choose it.

Let the truths we have considered move us to turn our faces toward heaven and bend our course in its direction. The desirableness of heaven ought to stir us to seek after it with all our heart. Upon hearing of this world of love, are you not weary of this present world of contention, confusion, calumny, and cruelty? Can you possibly be content in such a world? Who in their right mind would lay up treasures in this world? After all, treasures laid up for this world will never be enjoyed in hell.

In heaven we will find the rest that we crave. As we leave earth we will leave all our cares, troubles, fatigues, perplexities, and disturbances.

Let those who are poor and despised among men not be too bothered by these circumstances. But rather, seek heaven where there is no poverty or contempt, but where all are honored, esteemed, and loved by all. Do not hate others for their abusing you, but set your heart on heaven, that world of love.

Finally, let us consider some directions for seeking heaven.

First, do not let your heart go after the things of this world as your chief good. Do not indulge yourself in the possession of earthly things as if they could satisfy your soul, for that is the opposite of seeking heaven. You must not allow worldly pursuits to occupy your thoughts or time in heaping up the dust of the earth. Mortify desires for vain glory, and become poor in spirit.

Second, engage yourself often in conversing with heavenly persons, objects, and enjoyments. If you truly seek heaven, your thoughts will be there. Therefore, commune with the Triune God in prayer. Think and meditate much upon the God of love, the angels, and saints in the world of love, and the enjoyments and privileges there. Let your conversation be in heaven.

Third, be content to pass through all difficulties that lie in the path to heaven. The heavenly city is situated, as it were, on the top of a hill, and the only way to it is by many difficult steps upward. But what is all that in comparison with the sweet rest that awaits you at the end? The nearer you come to reaching that city, the more you will be cheered by the glorious prospects before you.

Fourth, keep your eyes fixed on the Lord Jesus Christ. He has entered into heaven as our forerunner. Think of Him. He is our righteousness to open the door to heaven. He is our mediator who ever lives to make to intercession for us. He is our example in patient endurance and great suffering. He is our strength who enables us to press on and conquer every foe. He is our surety that we shall inherit the blessed promises.

Fifth, if you would live forever in the world of love, live now a life of love—love to God and love to man. In this way we are like the souls already in heaven: we confirm what we profess, and we evidence our fitness for the world of love. As you live a life of love, you will find the windows of heaven opened and its light beaming into your soul. Soon the same grace that put heaven in your soul will take your soul to heaven. Happy, thrice happy, will you be when you enter into the joy of the Lord. What unspeakable bliss to know the reality of these words: "Behold, the tabernacle of God is with men, and he will dwell with them, and they shall be his people, and God himself shall be with them, and be their God. And God shall wipe away all tears from their eyes; and there shall be no more death, neither sorrow, nor crying, neither shall there be any more pain: for the former things are passed away" (Rev. 21:3–4)!

Recent Titles from Free Grace Press

The Exorcism of Satan: The Binding of the Strong Man by Christ the King

Joshua P. Howard

Series Editor, Owen Strachan

"Josh Howard addresses an important but often overlooked area of the study of the end times. Jesus has defeated Satan, and Scripture speaks of Satan as presently bound. But what exactly does this mean? Dr. Howard carefully analyzes the biblical teaching about the exorcism of our defeated foe—what Satan can and cannot do until the Lord's return. This is a thorough and compelling book that addresses and answers many of the questions students of eschatology have about this fascinating topic."

– Dr. Kim Riddlebarger, PhD

The Gospel Made Clear to Children

Jennifer Adams

Beautifully illustrated with short chapters, T*he Gospel Made Clear to Children* details the person and work of Christ. It begins with the holiness of God, the sinfulness of man, and the penalty for sin. It considers the love of God in eternity past and the provision God has made in sending His Son. It traces the incarnation, birth, life, and ministry of Jesus Christ, with a special focus on His crucifixion, resurrection, ascension, and exaltation. It culminates with a call to repent and believe, ending with the evidence of true conversion. Written from a heart full of love, this book calls children to turn from their sins and trust in Christ.

"The highest recommendation I can give to this wonderful book is that I will be reading it over and over again to my children. It is rich in biblical doctrine and is an invaluable instrument to aid parents in teaching their children the glorious truths of "God in Christ" reconciling the world to Himself. I know of no other book that so clearly communicates the great doctrines of the gospel to children."

– Paul Washer,
Author, Director of HeartCry Missionary Society

The Gospel Made Clear to Children Study Guide

Jennifer Adams

The Gospel Made Clear to Children Study Guide is to be used alongside *The Gospel Made Clear to Children* book. This companion guide takes a deeper look into the Scripture verses mentioned in the book. The study questions promote reflection and application, moving truth from the head to the heart. The goal is to help children be not only hearers of the Word but also doers. Each section ends with a brief prayer, encouraging children to ask the Lord for grace and help.

A Portrait of God: Stephen Charnock's Discourses upon the Existence and Attributes of God, Summarized for the 21st Century

Daniel Chamberlin

Stephen Charnock (1628-1680) wrote what is considered to be the fullest treatment of the attributes of God, even though he did not live to complete the treatise. It is truly a biblical portrait of God drawn with a Puritan pen, rightly deserving its place among the best of Puritan productions and of English literature altogether. However, today's reader may find the 1146 pages a bit daunting. This summary presents the treatise in a more manageable form that maintains the theological depth and practical application of the original. Don't miss out on the riches of Charnock!

Basic Christian Doctrines

Dr. Curt Daniel

Basic Christian Doctrines is very much what the title suggests—a concise introduction to the fundamental doctrines taught in the Bible. In fifty short chapters consisting of ten simple points each, Daniel presents a thorough introduction to evangelical Christian theology. Those who want a short and non-technical summary of basic Christian theology will find this an excellent tool for Sunday school classes, home Bible studies, homeschools and Christian high schools, and personal Bible study. *Basic Christian Doctrines* is an important, useful handbook every Christian should keep close at hand.

"Usually, other attempts to accomplish a work like this fall flat. Either the subjects are treated with far too much verbiage—thus unnecessarily lengthening the prose, or else easy enough to read but are much too elementary in content. Daniel, however, deftly succeeds with both aims where many other writers do not."

– *Dr. Lance Quinn,*
Executive Vice-President, The Expositors Seminary, Jupiter, FL

A Commentary on Galatians: Christ Plus Equals Nothing

Tom Nettles with Sylvia Nettles Dickson

Tom Nettles brings us a thought-provoking and thorough commentary on this important epistle by the apostle Paul to the church in Galatia, driving home the central theme of the glory of Christ in his perfect obedience to all the requirements of God's law. Christ Plus Equals Nothing is written in an easy-to-read outline format, sprinkled with insightful commentary from his sister, Sylvia Nettles Dickson.

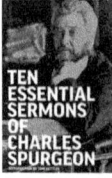

Ten Essential Sermons of Charles Spurgeon

Charles Spurgeon, with an introduction by Tom Nettles

"Charles Haddon Spurgeon had no peer in the theological density of his sermons. At the same time, he had no peer in their simplicity. He looked at truth, to which Christ came to bear witness and embody, as the pathway not only for altering the mind but for shaping the affections. These ten sermons exemplify this pattern of deep doctrine, simple but elegant and engaging presentation, and a call to faith and love. ...The effort to isolate ten influential sermons from a preacher who preached thousands of such sermons is daunting. These sermons, however, succeed in illustrating Spurgeon's doctrine, his evangelistic commitment, the beauty of his language, the manner in which a biblical text suggests a subject, and his passion for the glory of the triune God and the eternal well-being of souls."

– from the introduction by Tom Nettles

The Missionary Crisis: Five Dangers Plaguing Missions and How the Church Can Be the Solution

Paul Snider, foreword by Paul Washer

The Missionary Crisis confronts five dangers facing missionaries and the local churches that send them and gives biblical and practical instruction for missionaries, sending churches, and mission organizations. This book boldly approaches gentle correction for the missionary to reverse these five crises in their ministries. It challenges the local church to prepare and equip men and women for the high calling of missionary life.

"Paul Snider's book, *The Missionary Crisis*, is like looking through a window. He divulges the plight of modern missions with engaging reality. As a missionary, Paul's perspective will afford the reader a much greater concern for what is called today kingdom advancement. Years ago, a mission director said that "the mission field is littered with uncrucified flesh." His assessment, both then and now, is accurate. But Paul doesn't stop after exposing the encumbrances to global missions; he offers biblical and practical solutions to the problems. Local churches, mission agencies, and anyone with an interest in gospel mission enterprise will profit immensely from this superb work."

– Don Currin, HeartCry Missionary Society
Eastern European Coordinator

Visit
www.FreeGracePress.com
for these and many
other excellent resources.